In *Teaching Teenagers in a Post-Christian World*, Jake Kircher calls us to reset how we communicate the truth of Scripture to teenagers. We need to clear our memories and adapt our approach to their real world. It's not the world many of us grew up in. Jake's style is transparent and humble. He advocates an organic style of ministry that acknowledges and draws on the worldviews and learning styles of students. What he says should be carefully considered by youth leaders—especially those of us whose faith was nurtured in the "God said it...I believe it...that settles it" era. It's a helpful and provocative read.

Doug Clark
Director of Field Ministries
National Network of Youth M

As you read this book, you will hit bottom with Kircher and then begin to see youth ministry from a new perspective. It's a tough perspective. You can't just pour the essence of this book into your cup of ministry, add water, and stir. This is a call to leaders to give up all the superficialities, competitions, and idols of our present ministries and accept a radical relationship with Christ, with the intention of showing young people the difficult cost and high value of discipleship—a radical relationship with Jesus. Only this way can young people escape the limitations and bondage of a post-modern, post-Christian age. It is a self-critical approach to ministry—one in which we need to learn and determine our goals through self-reflection and out of deep relationships with youth, discovering with them what life is all about and how true, loving relationships grow. This book might be too searing and personal, a little too radical and honest for you—though I hope not; because it's also disarmingly practical.

Dean Borgman
Charles E. Culpeper Professor of Youth Ministries, Gordon-Conwell Theological Seminary
Founder and Director, Center for Youth Studies

How refreshing to get advice from someone who's right in the thick of the challenge of sharing faith with young people. Jake writes from the perspective of an experienced youth pastor who knows that the old methods of teaching teenagers are increasingly ineffective. The goal remains the same: for teenagers to develop a deep commitment to God that will last a lifetime. But standing up front at a youth meeting and telling teens what to believe isn't working. Instead, Jake gives us inspiration and practical guidance to teach teenagers who are immersed in modern culture and, of course, the digital world. This is a place where having the space to explore and ask questions is a critical element of the journey to truth, and Jake's advice will ring true to anyone wondering how to help young people find faith in a postmodern world.

Chris Curtis
CEO, Youthscape

Teaching Teenagers in a Post-Christian World is a quick but important read for far too many of us youth workers who declare we have a plan for ministering to youth, but deep down we aren't really sure that what we're accomplishing will last. Jake Kircher is not afraid to be honest about his youth ministry past and what he believes today.

Mike King
President, Youthfront
Author of *Presence-Centered Youth Ministry: Guiding Students into Spiritual Formation*
Twitter @MDKing

I loved this book and I highly recommend it. Jake Kircher understands today's culture and gives us wonderful insights on communicating with teenagers. This book is well researched and no doubt will give you many effective tools to speak to this generation.

Jim Burns, Ph.D.
President, HomeWord
Author of *Teenology* and *Confident Parenting*

Teaching Teenagers in a Post-Christian World is a must-read for youth workers who are in the trenches. Jake Kircher has written an honest and practical book full of thoughtful and deliberate strategies for guiding teenagers' spiritual formation in today's very complex, post-Christian world. Kircher can do this so well because he is immersed in this paradigm shift as he ministers to teens in the Northeast. His personal accounts resonate with my own and, most likely, with those of any youth worker who is passionate about leading students into life-giving faith. My recommendation is that you buy a copy of this book for yourself—and then buy six more!

Brock Morgan
Author of *Youth Ministry in a Post-Christian World*

Teaching is often missized in youth ministries. We either give it grandiose value, or we're entirely too dismissive of the power of the spoken Word. Jake Kircher is clearly a gifted practitioner, and he does a skillful job of right-sizing the importance of teaching in our ministries. This work is a masterful combination of stating the inaccuracies of our theology and practices, while offering creative, practical insights for how to do it better.

April L. Diaz
Author of *Redefining the Role of the Youth Worker*
The Youth Cartel's Director of Coaching
aprildiaz.com

Teaching Teenagers in a Post-Christian World is an engaging and compelling journey of ministry transformation with huge kingdom implications. I enjoyed Jake's personal, even vulnerable, approach as he moved his youth ministry to one characterized by "exploration and ownership." My favorite chapter is chapter 5, "Why We Discourage Exploration." We don't mean to, of course; but we end up, as he aptly describes it, making our students listeners, not livers of the Christian faith. I love how Jake's book is filled with fresh hope for youth ministry—and the whole church!

Len Kageler, Ph.D.
Professor of Youth and Family Studies, Nyack College
Author of *Youth Ministry in a Multifaith Society*

TEACHING TEENAGERS IN A POST-CHRISTIAN WORLD

CULTIVATING EXPLORATION AND OWNERSHIP

JAKE KIRCHER

TEACHING TEENAGERS IN A POST-CHRISTIAN WORLD

Publisher: Mark Oestreicher
Managing Editor: Laura Gross
Editor: Tamara Rice
Cover Design: Adam McLane
Layout: Marilee R. Pankratz
Creative Director: Mr. Holland

ISBN-13: 978-0-9910050-6-2
ISBN-10: 0991005066

The Youth Cartel, LLC
www.theyouthcartel.com
Email: info@theyouthcartel.com
Born in San Diego
Printed in the U.S.A.

To My Dad

Yours are still the only sermons I can remember from when I was a kid. Thanks for modeling the importance of always pointing people to Jesus. More so, thanks for showing me the necessity of diving into Scripture daily and exploring my faith. I will always have a picture in my mind of you sitting on the floor of your bedroom, underneath the air conditioner, reading your Bible.

CONTENTS

Foreword by Mark DeVries

Acknowledgements

Chapter 1	Something Needed to Change	23
Chapter 2	The Ultimate Goal	31
Chapter 3	The Importance of Exploration	47
Chapter 4	What Does Exploration Look Like?	61
Chapter 5	Why We Discourage Exploration	79
Chapter 6	The Vision We Are Passing On	97

Suggested Resources 103

Endnotes 105

FOREWORD

When it concerns our spiritual lives,
the answers often get in the way.
Because once we have answers and words,
it's a closed subject.

— Mark Yaconelli

For the last two summers, we've done something a little bit odd with our graduating seniors.

For well over a decade, we had a tradition of taking our graduates on a trip by themselves. It's become an amazing rite of passage, one that moves our teens from being recipients of ministry to being partners in the gospel. But here's what's been odd over these past two years…

We've moved away from having our staff give a talk each night. For our teens, this was a huge step. We've got a team of amazing communicators, and our group loves to learn from them. But we decided we wouldn't teach on this trip—at least not in the traditional way.

We still had a time of worship, but the focus of our evening programs was…well, to provoke doubt. Rather than bolstering our kids with more of "our answers," we decided we'd demonstrate our confidence in the durability of the gospel by inviting them to express their dormant doubts, which hide so easily in the fog of a mission-camp high.

So we had them read a little Dostoyevsky, a little Bonhoeffer, a little Anne Lamott—each one triggered bigger questions than most of these teenagers had ever considered. And we adults voiced our own doubts as well, hoping to inoculate the young people against the paralysis that so easily overcomes those who are facing questions they can't answer for the first time.

I know what you're wondering: *Did it work? Did anyone doubt your sanity? Did you get fired?*

The quick answer is that the young people who went on these trips will consistently look back on that week as one of the most profoundly faith-shaping weeks of their lives. It was enough to make us ask why.

THE OPPOSITE OF FAITH?

Among other things, the book you now hold in your hands makes a strong case that as we teach our teenagers, we must remember that doubt is not the enemy of faith—although certainty might be. Jake may startle you as he advocates moving students beyond the "certainty" of answers by adopting a way of teaching that invites the unsettledness that awakens real faith.

It's true that certainty has a way of keeping our faith stable, if somewhat domesticated. But doubt can quickly become the ants in the pants of our spiritual lives. We don't have to read too far into Jesus' story to see his peculiar way of decentering his listeners, of tossing them into water that is way over their heads.

It is no small thing that Oswald Chambers, author of *My Utmost for His Highest*—perhaps the most influential book of devotions ever written, said, "Doubt is not always a sign that a man is thinking wrong; it may be a sign that he is thinking."[i] And Scott Peck echoes this idea: "Individuals remain stuck... precisely because they do not doubt deeply enough."[ii]

We'd do well to remember that the Pharisees had answers while the disciples—whom God used to change the world—were full of questions.

C. S. Lewis has provided countless Christians with "answers" to some of the most difficult questions of the Christian faith. But at the same time, he wrote:

> It is a profound mistake to imagine that Christianity ever intended to dissipate the bewilderment...*It comes to intensify [it]*....Many a man, brought up in the glib profession of some shallow form of Christianity, who comes through reading Astronomy to realise for the first time how majestically indifferent most reality is to man, and who perhaps abandons his religion on that account, may at that moment be having his first genuinely religious experience.[iii] (emphasis mine)

When it comes to this tension between certainty and doubt, I return again and again to a beautiful story I've heard told about a time when someone asked Mother Teresa for prayer:

> When the brilliant ethicist John Kavanaugh went to

work for three months at "the house of the dying" in Calcutta, he was seeking a clear answer as to how best to spend the rest of his life. On the first morning there he met Mother Teresa. She asked, "And what can I do for you?" Kavanaugh asked her to pray for him.

"What do you want me to pray for?" she asked. He voiced the request that he had borne thousands of miles from the United States. "Pray that I have clarity."

She said firmly, "No, I will not do that." When he asked her why, she said, "Clarity is the last thing you are clinging to and must let go of." When Kavanaugh commented that *she* always seemed to have the clarity he longed for, she laughed and said, "I have never had clarity; what I have always had is trust. So I will pray that you trust God."[iv]

Could it be that our traditional teaching methods are actually impeding teens' progress in Christ? Could it be that our strong commitment to "core content" may be keeping young people from engaging the claims of Christ with all of their minds? Could it be that our best efforts may be insulating teenagers from asking the very questions that hold the greatest promise of driving them "further up and further in"?[v] (Thank you, Reepicheep!)

THE PURPOSE OF TEACHING

I remember reading the transcript of a teenager being interviewed for one of the many research projects on faith retention in America. The conversation went like this:

Interviewer: Is there any difference between the way you live your life and the way your non-Christian friends live their lives?
Student: No, everyone is the same.
Interviewer: So why are you a Christian?
Student: It's how I was raised.
Interviewer: Anything else?
Student: No.
Interviewer: But being a Christian is important to you?
Student: Absolutely.
Interviewer: Why?
Student: My youth pastor is awesome.[vi]

I have to admit that, if I'm not careful, the goal of my teaching can easily be reduced to nothing greater than having teenagers (or their parents or the pastor or the board) think I am a good, engaging, and orthodox communicator. In short, I'd love for the students in my youth group to think, *My youth pastor is awesome!*

We've got more (and better) resources at our fingertips than ever before. We've got better PowerPoint presentations and videos. We've got more mnemonic devices (think "The three Cs of transformation") and acrostics (did you know that each letter of the word "RELATIONSHIPS" stands for something?)—and all of them are designed to help us share *our content* more effectively.

But is it possible that although we may be growing more impressive as communicators, our youth are retaining little more than our impressiveness? Is it possible that declaring the gospel might take place the best when we're *listening*, not talking?

I've been wondering lately what might happen if we asked our confirmation students to write their "Statements of Doubt" *before* they write their statements of faith. I wonder if we aren't creating an environment (albeit unintentionally) in which young people develop a faith in their own faith, rather than a faith in God, because they learn from us to limit their faith in Christ to knowing the answers. The result of this approach seems to be spiritually fragile high school graduates who are easily overwhelmed whenever they find themselves in the crucible of doubt.

BRINGING IT HOME

I heard an interesting complaint about one of our mission camps recently. The teens had grown accustomed to one of our staff people "bringing it home" with a powerful message on the last night of camp. But for our recent graduates, we'd decided to forgo the emotional ending of the week and instead invited them to encounter God on their own—"without training wheels."

Some said they missed the emotions of the last night of camp. They missed the chance to recommit their lives to Christ "in the heat of the moment." They missed hearing a strong challenge from a great communicator.

And, frankly, we did too.

But we decided nothing could "bring it home" more profoundly for these young adults than "putting the fork in their hands."

Teaching Teenagers in a Post-Christian World has raised all kinds of questions in me:

- What would happen if we devoted the same amount of time that we now spend creating great outlines and illustrations and instead invented ways to provoke our kids to think?
- What would happen if our youth group meetings became the most fascinating place in town for unbelieving teens to raise their real-life questions?
- What if there were a way to teach that would equip our young people to bring their friends to Christ themselves, not just invite friends to church or youth group so they can listen to "an expert" who has all the answers?
- What would happen if our youth began tweeting each other's brilliant insights and questions, rather than the words of the "sage on the stage"?
- What if we put the fork in our students' hands and trusted that the Spirit is at work in their questions and that God and God's people are not freaked out by honest questions like "How long?" and "Why?" and "Who says…?"

Our friends at Sticky Faith estimate "that seven of every ten students is struggling with doubts—but only one or two of those ten is likely to have had conversations about those doubts with youth leaders or friends during high school."[vii] If Jake's book does its work, you may wind up with more questions than answers. I think he might have planned it that way.

May those questions drive you deeper into the heart of the One who was fearless in the face of questions, who is big enough to delight in our doubts, and who dreams greater dreams for our teenagers than we can ever imagine.

Mark DeVries
Founder, Ministry Architects
Associate Pastor for Youth and Their Families
First Presbyterian Church
(Nashville, Tennessee) 1986–2014

[i] Jim Thomas, *Coffeehouse Theology: Where Real Questions Meet Honest Answers* (Eugene: OR, Harvest House, 2000), 111.
[ii] M. Scott Peck, M.D., *The Different Drum: Community Making and Peace* (New York: Simon & Schuster, 1988), 201).
[iii] C. S. Lewis, *Miracles* (New York: HarperCollins, 1996), 81.
[iv] Brennan Manning, Ruthless Trust: The Ragamuffin Path to God (New York: HarperCollins, 2000), 5.
[v] C. S. Lewis, *The Last Battle* (New York: HarperCollins, 1984), chapter 16.
[vi] Kenda Creasy Dean, OMG: A Youth Ministry Handbook (Nashville: Abingdon Press, 2010), 10.
[vii] Brad M. Griffin and Kara Powell, "I Doubt It: Allowing Space for Questions," Fuller Youth Institute, Sticky Faith, http://stickyfaith.org/articles/i-doubt-it.

ACKNOWLEDGEMENTS

A huge thank you goes out to Marko and The Youth Cartel for buying into the vision of this book and taking a chance with its content. I got a lot of nos from others with this material, and I thank you profusely for your yes! Thanks to Adam, Laura, Tamara, and Marilee for your hard work to make this book the best it could be.

Thanks to my wife Melissa for supporting me, putting up with me talking about ideas and stories, and giving me extra time to write. This book would not be a reality without your love, encouragement, and help.

Thanks to Mark Orr (New England's Marko!) for your mentorship, prayer, listening ear, and friendship. There is no way I would still be in ministry if it weren't for you. Thank you for being the first one willing to read the manuscript and give me feedback. Your encouragement keeps me going like no one else's in ministry.

Thanks to Patti, Scott, Brittany, and Abby for taking the time to read my first drafts and give me feedback.

Thanks to my church, Grace Community Church in New Canaan, for giving me the space to explore new styles of teaching with our students, which brings me to a HUGE thanks to my students for showing up week after week and challenging me to communicate more and more effectively about Jesus and faith. Thanks for pushing me, asking great questions, and allowing me to do the same to you. Thanks for being brave enough to tell me when you thought I was stupid to believe what I believe.

Thanks to my local youth worker network. I love praying, worshiping, and talking faith with all of you. Thanks for the space to vent, to question, and to explore faith deeper in a setting where I don't have to worry about being fired for what I say or ask. Thanks for your partnership in changing our area for Christ and reaching more and more students and their families with the gospel.

Thanks to Starbucks and Dunkin' Donuts for your free Wi-Fi and the space to write. Thanks to Hillsong United, All Sons & Daughters, Demon Hunter, and Eminem for providing the soundtrack as I wrote.

SOMETHING NEEDED TO CHANGE CHAPTER 1

In my first 12 years of youth ministry, the programs and meetings I ran would always have that special moment when I'd stand up and tell my students everything I knew about Jesus. I'd use video clips, skits, object lessons, songs, and anything else I could think of to complement what I was speaking on that week. But more than anything else, I'd just get up and TEACH.

Honestly, I think I'm pretty good at that sort of thing. I, like some of you, consider the gift of teaching to be one of my biggest strengths and spiritual gifts. And on top of that, I've worked hard to hone my teaching skills by taking all the right classes in college, reading a number of books on the topic, and even attending numerous conference workshops on speaking. Throughout the years, parents and students usually complimented me after my talks ("That was great!"), and from week to week teens kept coming back for more. But during that same time frame, a growing wave of frustration made me doubt my effectiveness as a Bible teacher.

As I spent time with students outside of youth group over coffee or pizza (or any other staple food group of youth ministry), they would always ask me questions, and these questions, much of the time, had already been answered in that "great talk" I'd just given. (Which made me feel like they weren't really listening, even though I knew they were.) I began to feel like all my great teaching and perfectly executed theological explanations were going in one ear and out the other.

Beyond the deeper questions that were being asked by regulars, I also started to realize a number of the students coming to our youth group didn't even have a basic understanding of Christian beliefs. I remember a seventh grader named Nick who attended an outreach event where the gospel was clearly communicated. At the end of the message, he decided to respond to the speaker's invitation to "come forward and receive Christ." Once those who'd come forward were assembled in a back room, the speaker even re-explained the gospel and led them in the "Sinner's Prayer." As I walked out of the room with Nick, I was on cloud nine. I was only 19, and it was my first gig as a youth pastor. (Nick was one of the first students to start a relationship with Jesus on my watch!)

But my spiritual high crashed pretty quickly when we got outside and Nick asked, "Jake, what's sin?" It suddenly dawned on me that the speaker, even though he went through the gospel twice, never actually explained what sin was. He'd just assumed it was common knowledge. When I turned to Nick and wondered aloud if he'd understood anything the speaker had explained, he just beamed at me and answered, "Nope."

Then there was Dan, a ninth grader who had grown up in Austria with very little church background and had been coming to our youth group for a number of months. One Monday night at our youth group meeting, I was moving along in the talk and made a casual reference to the disciples. Pretty quickly, Dan's hand shot up and he asked, "Wait...what are disciples?" (He didn't even know they were people!)

More recently, during one of our services I was teaching on the David and Goliath story. Afterward, a student came up to me and said, "Dude! I've always wanted to know where the idea of a David facing Goliath came from. I always hear it on ESPN in reference to a huge upset by an underdog, but I never knew why. Now I do. Thanks!"

And my favorite? I once asked a group of students to name a person from the Bible who ignored God's plan and instead did what he wanted to. I was looking for someone to respond that it was Jonah, of course. Instead, a high school girl raised her hand and said, "It's the Veggie Tales guy who is an asparagus... and there's a tree that dies."

It used to be that pretty much every student who walked into a church had some basic knowledge of the Bible and the core beliefs of Christianity. But in an increasingly post-Christian culture, that basic knowledge of Scripture and Christianity is becoming more and more the exception.[1] This is especially true in New England, where I've lived and worked my whole life, as well as in much of the Western United States. Many youth workers today are trying to reach students who are third-generation unchurched. If you're from the Bible Belt, you may be seeing this only minimally right now. But I can guarantee that wherever you're ministering, this unchurched phenomenon will eventually begin to surface.

When you look at the history of Israel in the Old Testament or at the pattern of spiritual revival and decline since the New Testament church, you can pick up on a common trend:

Generally after a few generations of deep faith, people forget what God has done and drift away from him. While the United States has experienced several significant periods of Christian revival, starting with the First Great Awakening in New England during the 1700s, we're arguably in decline right now in many parts of the country. Between this spiritual decline and our dwindling Recession-era church budgets, many of us have had to re-examine how we do church, but it's particularly our new post-Christian context that has become a reality for many youth workers, including me.

So in the midst of processing my students' increasing lack of what we in the church call Christian education, I quickly ran into another issue that eventually affects every veteran youth worker: My students were graduating, heading off to college, and seemingly losing interest in their faith. I'd check in with former students or see them during school breaks, and our interactions became incredibly predictable. When I'd ask where they were at with Jesus, it was like listening to a recording. They weren't going to any church because they couldn't find one, didn't like what they had found, or were so busy with school and their social lives that they just wanted to sleep in on Sundays. (Yes, I did tell them some churches have evening services on Saturday or Sunday night, but it didn't make a difference.) Some had read bits and pieces of the devotional we gave them as a gift when they graduated, but most hadn't cracked their Bibles at all. To top it all off, many weren't interested in coming to church again—even once they were back home.

Around that same time, a number of books that dealt with this topic started to come out. *Soul Searching* by Christian Smith and Melinda Lundquist Denton was one of the first, and the authors concluded through their research that many Christian teens didn't even have a faith in Jesus per se. Instead, the young people in the study believed in what the authors called Moralistic Therapeutic Deism. (As in, being a good person, doing what makes you happy, and believing God created everything but isn't really involved anymore.)

Shortly after that, two other books hit the market that looked at the other side of the issue: how young adults felt about their faith and the church as a whole. In response to *They Like Jesus but Not the Church* by Dan Kimball and *unChristian* by David Kinnaman and Gabe Lyons, there seemed to be a hyperfocus on how youth ministries, and those who ran them, had failed to teach our teens and what we needed to start doing differently. It wasn't until more recently with Kenda Creasy Dean's *Almost Christian*, along with *Sticky Faith* by Kara Powell and Chap Clark, that this issue became elevated to more of an overall church problem, instead of just a youth ministry problem.

Prior to *Almost Christian* and *Sticky Faith*, it was frustrating to me that so many people knew about the problem, yet so few seemed to have any solutions. And the few small solutions being offered were shot down by my senior pastor and church leadership at the time, compounding my frustration even more. I remember getting to a point where I walked out of a general session at a youth ministry conference, because I was so completely tired of hearing speakers say the same things over and over again. I was also tired of feeling like a failure, even though I was trying the best I could to help teenagers realize a deeper faith.

With each year in ministry, my frustrations continued to grow as the interactions with my students, both current and graduated, seemed to increasingly follow these same patterns. Everything was eventually pushed over the edge for me, however, while on a student mission trip to Chicago. During a debriefing discussion one evening, we were unpacking some of the teens' interactions with a few homeless people, and the conversation turned to the topic of evangelism and sharing our faith. I casually threw out an (almost) rhetorical question, assuming it would be quickly answered in good Sunday school fashion, but I wasn't prepared for their response. "What's the gospel?" I asked, and—to my shock—my question was met with blank stares.

Now, these teenagers were *not* unchurched students on a mission trip for the first time. These teens were regulars in our programs, and some were even on our student leadership team and had solid Christian parents who were heavily involved in our church as leaders themselves. They were at church and youth group weekly and had heard numerous talks discussing sin, the incarnation, Christ's death and resurrection, and the redemptive work of grace. Yet not one of them was able to clearly outline the gospel without prompts and coaching from me.

I felt like the biggest ministry failure that night. My dad, who is also a pastor, had always taught me that communicating the gospel was the most important part of teaching, and it's something I'd taken to heart in my ministry. So at that moment I felt like my years in ministry had just been a complete waste of everyone's time.

With my frustrations at a head, I came back from Chicago believing I was done with ministry. Right before the trip, I'd been approached by a teen mentoring organization without any religious affiliation, and they wanted me to consider applying for their director position. When we got back, I went ahead and submitted my résumé for the job.

I obviously wasn't being effective in what I was doing at the church, and I knew something needed to change.

CHAPTER 2

Sometimes God purposefully allows us to get to a low point because it's such an effective way to prompt stubborn people to change. With my résumé submitted for the new job and a friend on the search committee (the same one who begged me to apply in the first place, saying I was a "perfect fit"), I figured I was a shoo-in for the position at the mentoring organization and could soon leave all my ministry frustrations behind. However, it turns out God had different plans because I never even got a call to interview.[2]

Changing my external setting would've been the easy fix, but God had no intention of letting me take the easy way out. Instead, he wanted me to dig deeper into the issues I was facing and bring about a fundamental change in the way I thought about teaching teenagers, particularly in light of the increasingly post-Christian world outside my church doors, which impacts my students far more hours each week than I ever could.

Realizing I was stuck in ministry, I started praying and purposefully wrestling with the question of what I could do differently to more effectively communicate Jesus' amazing story of grace and love. But almost immediately, I saw that wasn't the first thing I needed to ask myself. I couldn't change my methodology without going one question deeper: *What was the whole point of teaching in the first place?*

It may seem like an odd question at first glance, but I quickly learned that the answer to this question (and more importantly, how we live out that answer) is crucial to reaching people with the gospel in a post-Christian world.

Take a minute and consider how you'd answer the question: *What's the point of teaching?*

To help people understand the Bible?

To understand Jesus' teachings?

To make sure people know the right way to live? (And thus by association the wrong way to live as well?)

To challenge people's beliefs?

These are the answers I would have given a few years ago, and they are by no means *bad* answers. However, I've to come to believe they actually fall short of the ultimate goal that should be at the forefront of teaching.

WHAT WOULD JESUS DO?

Author and speaker Francis Chan once asked youth workers at a conference, "If Jesus was a youth pastor, would your kids go to his youth group? Would you?" Frankly (and unfortunately), I think the answer to this question is no. In fact, I think if Jesus were a youth worker or pastor today, he'd get fired pretty quickly.

By our standards, Jesus was a horrible teacher. He didn't have perfectly molded lessons with three specific points. He didn't have clever hooks or easy to understand sayings or acronyms. His points didn't always start with the same letter. Instead, his teaching was often confusing, frustrating, short, and a huge turnoff. More often than not, it seems to me the crowds flocked to Jesus because of his signs and wonders; but then when Jesus taught, people tended to walk away and never come back. After three grueling years of ministry, Jesus, the Son of God incarnate, had a following of only 120 people![3]

Was Jesus purposefully trying to confuse people?

Was he trying to hide the gospel from them?

Obviously not. Instead, I think he was inviting the disciples and the crowds to enter into a conversation. He wanted them to open their hearts and minds to the things of God and to experience a real relationship with him.

Jesus could have just given the answers clearly and in easy to understand ways. He could have pulled out his flannelgraph and waxed eloquent, explaining the Romans Road and watching droves come down the aisles for an altar call. But instead, Jesus seemed to understand something we tend to overlook.

The people didn't need answers—they had plenty of those from the religious teachers. What people needed was a *relationship* with The Answer. Consider what Jesus leads with when he starts his teaching ministry. It's not an expository look at Old

Testament law. It's not an in-depth exploration of popular theological stances of the day. It's a simple one-liner that says it all: "Repent, for the kingdom of heaven has come near" (Matt. 4:17).

This same teaching was preached by John the Baptist prior to Jesus beginning his ministry; however, there's a major difference in what Jesus is getting at here. Consider this note from *The Expositor's Bible Commentary* (emphasis added):

> When John the Baptist says these words, they are placed in an [Old Testament] context that highlights his function as the forerunner who looks forward to the Messiah and his kingdom; when Jesus says the same words, they are linked with an [Old Testament] context that *insists Jesus fulfills the promises*.[4]

Jesus is calling people to himself—not to a theology, not to a denomination, not to a church, an organization, or even a religion. He is saying to turn around (aka repent) from everything else and instead look to him, the bodily fulfillment of God's kingdom on earth. He drives this stake of truth in even deeper starting in Matthew 4, where he goes out and calls his first disciples to follow *him*.

It's important to understand who these disciples were, too: fishermen, tax collectors, and zealots. Jesus wasn't calling the best of the best to follow him. He wasn't calling the "good" religious people. He was calling rabbinical school flunkouts and the outcasts of society. They were the dirty, the hated, and the disregarded that no one would have looked to for religious advice. Because the crux of Jesus' teaching as he started his ministry had everything to do with helping people understand *who they were* in regard to Christ. He valued them as creations of his Father and not because of what they did, what grades they got in Hebrew school, or how religious they were.

Yes, Jesus *does* care about how we live our lives. Matthew 5–7 shows that throughout the Sermon on the Mount as Jesus challenges the common practices of the time and calls the people to live differently. But it's not a coincidence that he spends the first part of that sermon telling the people who they are: blessed, salt, and light. *Then* he dives into what they should be doing differently.

Paul followed the same pattern in the book of Ephesians. Consider how a recent blog post explains this:

> The apostle Paul writes a letter to his friends in the city of Ephesus and for the first three chapters he doesn't tell them one thing to do. He simply tells them who they are in this new reality of Christ. He says they're blessed and adopted and redeemed and forgiven and included and marked and sealed and alive and raised up and on and on he goes, announcing who they are and what God has done for them and how Spirit now dwells in their midst.
>
> And then, in chapter 4, he begins to tell them what it practically looks like to live out this new reality in everyday life.

First, he tells them who they are,
then he tells them what to do.

Why?

Because the Jesus message is first and foremost an announcement of who you are. It's about your identity, about the new word that has been spoken about you, the love that has always been yours.

If you start with instructions and commands, people might be mistaken into thinking that God loves us because of what we do or how religious or moral or good we are. That's not gospel. Gospel is the announcement of who God insists you now are because of Christ. You're a child of God, not because of how great you are but because God has all kinds of kids and you're one of them.

But if you tell people who they are, who their best selves are, if you remind them of their true identity, there's a good chance they'll know what to do as they live out of that good news.[5]

At its deepest level, the point of teaching is to first and foremost point people towards an encounter, and subsequently into a relationship, with Jesus. It's to help people understand their worth and value in the eyes of Jesus. This is not to suggest that we never challenge people's actions or call into question how they are living, but this must be a secondary goal and not where we start.

PUTTING THE CART BEFORE THE HORSE

I love the line in Gungor's song "Cannot Keep You" off their album *Beautiful Things*:

We cannot keep you in a church
We cannot keep you in a Bible
Or it's just another idol to box you in[6]

The problem typically befalling teachers is that we fail to connect our listeners with Jesus and instead connect them to a theology, a book, a denomination, or a church. Those things aren't bad in and of themselves, but when they become the forefront or purpose of what we do in ministry, as Gungor bluntly puts it, the result is nothing short of idolatry.

For many, this idolatry wasn't necessarily intended, but we must be more purposeful in our teaching and ask some tough questions about what we're really winning people *to*. This is particularly important as we minister to those in a post-Christian culture, specifically the teens in our youth groups and young adults under 30. They have built-in crap detectors[7], and they are the first to be turned off when they feel like they are just a number or a consumer and not people we care for authentically. It's why people like Julia Duin, author of *Quitting Church*, told *YouthWorker.com* back in 2008 that if things continued to progress as they had been, the church in America would decrease by half before 2023.[8]

Shouldn't the goal of any teaching—whether live, online, or in book form—be to reach people with the message of the gospel and help grow *the Church*, not one's individual organization or denomination? James warns about this kind of behavior in his letter to early Christ followers, saying, "If you harbor bitter envy and selfish ambition in your hearts, do not boast about it or deny the truth. Such 'wisdom' does not come down from heaven but is earthly, unspiritual, demonic. For where you have envy and selfish ambition, there you find disorder and every evil practice" (James 3:14-16). When we put ourselves, our organization, our denomination, or our specific theology first in our teaching, we miss the point—and we can be sure our students and listeners will miss the point as well.

It seems to me that many of the conversations we have in the church today about helping people encounter Jesus are focused on church programs and gatherings, and subsequently having the right people in place to attract others to *come*. But isn't the whole point of evangelism that the Church needs to get out of its buildings, programs, and services and *go* to the people within our communities? (See the Great Commission in Matthew 28:18-20.)

This issue reveals the bad ecclesiology many Christ followers have. We often distort the idea of what a biblical church is. Jesus never wanted us to attract a bunch of non-Christians to some building, meeting, or organization. He wanted us as people and his body to be an attraction outside of our church's walls, and he wanted himself to shine through us where we all work, live, play, shop, and do life together.

This was exactly what Jesus modeled in his own ministry. He didn't set up a tent somewhere and invite everyone to come out for a revival every Friday night. Instead, he went to where the people were. He sent his disciples out, untrained and confused as they all were, to spread his message so people would know Jesus. The early church began not because everyone was invited to an outreach event, but because the disciples were out living life together when the Holy Spirit moved through them (Acts 2).

CONSUMER CHRISTIANITY

Once we flip the beginning of the Great Commission on its head and focus all our efforts on creative teaching that draws people to our churches and services, too often the result is that we create consumers rather than disciples.

Bill Hybels—once a youth pastor himself—famously began asking his surrounding community in the early 1970s why they weren't coming to church. The information he gathered is widely credited with shaping the youth and adult ministries at Willow Creek Church, which then grew exponentially. So one of my earliest attempts to rethink my teaching and make it more effective involved giving this "ask the people what they want" approach a try with our teenagers. We began asking them what we could change about our youth program to make church more comfortable for their friends.

The problem I ran into was that everyone answered our question based on what they personally wanted, and the responses I got were all over the place, many actually contradicted one another.

One teen would tell me we needed to have more music, and another would tell me to ditch the music altogether and have more games. Another student suggested shorter teaching times, and someone else said I needed to go deeper when I taught.

My leaders and I did our best to work with the many ideas we were given, but what we found was that none of them seemed to work. Even worse, we started to realize that many of the teenagers we'd approached with our question had stopped coming. Eventually our high school program dwindled down to a core group of about 10 teenagers. Week after week it seemed we had the same handful of teens at youth group having great conversations and deep discussions, but they hardly ever did this with their friends from outside the church.

After a few weeks of this, I was really thankful for Nich, one of my seniors at the time, who sat me down and told me what was going wrong with our strategy. First, he explained that although our question about how to make the youth group more inviting for their friends wasn't a bad question, it made some of our students feel used. They didn't feel like we, as a youth ministry, were caring for them as individuals anymore. Instead, it seemed like they were just the bricks we needed to build a bigger program. In other words, we were unintentionally telling teens they were nothing more than a means to an end, not children of a God who loves them unconditionally.

Second, Nich shared from his own experience that his friends lived too far away from the church for him to invite them. They simply weren't going to come to youth group from an hour away no matter what we changed. This made me think about some of the other teenagers who were coming from towns almost as far away as Nich's friends, and how their friends weren't likely to come that far either. Suddenly this new perspective made me feel like growing our ministry would be impossible.

As I shared this sinking feeling, as well as my heart to help teenagers reach their friends with Jesus' story, Nich challenged my thoughts and actually flipped the whole conversation around. During the time that we'd been focused on getting our students to bring their friends to our program so they could hear about Christ, Nich had been taking what was discussed at youth group on Sunday nights and having some great conversations with his friends around the lunch table and in the classroom throughout the week. Nich had brought Christ to them, which was actually what our goal in teaching should have been all along. When we help people understand their identity in Christ, they will naturally want to turn around and help others understand that same identity. (We'll dive deeper into the spiritual significance of identity in chapter 3.)

After charging his followers to "go" in the Great Commission, Jesus' next command is to "make disciples." This connects all the way back to the beginning of Matthew 4 where Jesus calls his first disciples. Jesus wants all people everywhere to follow him so closely that they begin to act, speak, and think just like him, and he wants the Church to model this.

I think this is the other thing Jesus is getting at in the Great Commission, when he tells us to baptize them "in the name of the Father and of the Son and of the Holy Spirit" (Matt. 28:19). Looking at the original language of this passage, we find something rather thought-provoking about these commands.

The Greek word *baptizo* ("to baptize") implies a repeated dipping or immersion, and the Greek word for *name* in this verse (as in, "in the name of...") was understood to be something much deeper than just a title for someone. *Onoma* ("name") represented everything a person was about: their character, interests, authority, deeds, wants, desires, etc. When we talk about the *onoma* of the Father, Son, and Holy Spirit, we're communicating so much more than just the literal names of the Trinity; we're referencing the character of God as *manifested* in the Trinity.

So, could it be that Jesus is saying to Christians in Matthew 28:19 that we are meant to go live our lives in such a way that we *immerse* people every day in *him*?[9]

Sadly, it seems to me that a lot of church growth comes about because Christians decide the new church down the street is better than the church they're already attending. It also seems to me that sometimes this happens solely because of a strategy, marketing campaign, or advertisement from this new church meant to win people over, which only fuels a consumerist approach to spirituality.

When we focus the majority of church time, energy, and money on new buildings, cool programs, trendy music styles, and wow-factor sermons, the focus shifts from Jesus to keeping people happy and entertained.

On top of being the epitome of bad ecclesiology, this shift away from encountering Jesus also puts the priesthood of believers (1 Peter 2:5) in peril, which has three unfortunate consequences for our students:

1. This shift tells teens that sharing Jesus with their friends should be left to the professionals.

Rather than using our teaching to help teenagers understand their value in Christ and empower them to live that out by offering their peers that same message at the lunch table, at work, on the athletic field, or at home, we tell the teens in our churches to just "bring a friend to church." (That's a theologically flawed statement, by the way.)

By focusing so much on "bring a friend to church" and creating outreach events where students bring their peers to hear about Jesus, we're subconsciously teaching them that sharing about Jesus should be left to the trained professionals. (Which, subsequently, is telling them they aren't good enough, talented enough, or trained enough to do it in the first place—thus contradicting the entire message of Jesus.) For teens coming from a post-Christian perspective, this damaging methodology goes a step further in that it not only tells them they aren't good enough, but it also ignores their cries to be a part of something meaningful.

2. This shift prevents many students from learning how to share their faith.

My favorite teacher was Mr. Keeney. I had him for three years of math during high school, and he always used to tell us, "Hear it, learn it once. Do it, learn it twice. Teach it, learn it for good." And that was how he ran his classes. We'd listen to him teach it. Then we'd do a worksheet and practice it ourselves. And then he'd put us in groups where we had to explain the math processes to each other. Math was the only high school subject I got straight As in every year, and a lot of that was because of Mr. Keeney and this model.

When it comes to the church, we tend to do really well with the first step. In most cases those coming to our churches and youth ministries hear all about Jesus and the Bible. However, because they view our meetings in a consumerist way as places to be entertained and get their Jesus quota for the week, the message stops there. If our teens do think about sharing their faith with their friends, it's normally out of some perceived requirement to be a "good" Christian and keep their parents or pastor happy. Then when they decide to try talking to a peer, many don't have the faintest idea about how to do it in a way that actually connects with their non-Christian friends.

3. This shift robs teenagers of the experience and joy of participating in God's kingdom work.

Lastly, I believe the church has done a cruel thing by stealing the joy of sharing Jesus with other people. As youth workers, we get to celebrate with our staff and volunteers whenever teens respond to the gospel. We send email reports to our senior pastors and boards with these encouraging stories. We go home to our spouses excited about what God has done through our talks. But shouldn't all Christians get to celebrate this joy, rather than just being happy they brought a friend to church or youth group to hear *us* give the gospel message? Our teenagers should get to experience the satisfaction and sense of deeper purpose that comes from doing God's work themselves. They should be able to feel firsthand the purpose and value they have within his kingdom.

Ultimately, failure to look at the core purpose of teaching as anything other than helping people encounter Jesus is only going to set up our churches—more specifically, our youth—for catastrophe down the road. I believe people are going to care increasingly less about the Church in a post-Christian world, especially if the Church is just another subculture trying to claim their attention, time, and money.

Now that we've set this new foundation for teaching, we can begin looking at our methodology.

Eventually, I started asking for thoughts and opinions from various people about what I could do differently in my teaching to help our teens encounter Jesus and discover their worth in him. One of the first leaders I approached for ideas was my senior pastor. After I explained everything going on in my heart and mind, he suggested I try something fairly simple. (To be honest, I initially hated his advice.)

His recommendation was to stop teaching every week and instead focus on letting the teens talk through and explore everyday issues and the implications their theology had on each one. Rather than telling teenagers what to believe or explaining what the Bible says on a particular issue, he suggested letting the young people share their own opinions. Then, according to him, after pointing to different Scripture passages relevant to the conversation, I could ask them to clarify what they were hearing and allow them to disagree and challenge one another.

Sure, this was the kind of thing I'd do when I met with students one on one or in a small group, but I'd never done it at youth group with everyone there. That was my time to teach, be up front, and give The Answers. This other approach would mean losing my role as Wise Teacher. (And, frankly, it was a role that made me feel really good about myself.)

But as I began working though this issue in my own heart, I was challenged by a simple realization: This new way coincided exactly with what Jesus did with his disciples and with larger groups. More often than not, he used stories and parables that didn't always make immediate sense. He used experiences that challenged the popular ways of thinking. And at the deepest level, he put people in situations where they had to question their previous conceptions about God, faith, and life, and explore other possibilities of truth.

Going back to the Great Commission, it's only *after* we're told to go out into the world, and *after* we're told to help people understand that Jesus loves and values them for who they are and not for what they do, and *after* we live in such a way that attracts people to Jesus and nothing else—that's when Jesus tells us to teach them "to observe all that I have commanded you" (Matt. 28:20 ESV).[10] I love the way the ESV translates the Greek word *tereo* as *observe* (it literally means "to watch" or "attend to carefully"), because I think it brings out the Jewish practice of teaching so well.

And who were the teachers of Jesus' day? Rabbis. And what was their main method of teaching? They'd have people follow them around, watching and listening to everything they did until the people learned to do the same things on their own. Wasn't that exactly what Jesus did with his disciples as they followed him around? Even in the way he taught people to live differently, it wasn't about giving them a specific theology or a denominational set of dos and don'ts within a classroom setting. Instead, it was about Jesus inviting them to observe and explore how he lived, and challenging them to go and do likewise.

The other element we need to consider is what Jesus meant by the phrase "all that I have commanded you" (Matt. 28:20 ESV). At first glance, this seems like the time to dive into the Bible to find a list of rules that are supposed to help people understand how to live and how not to live—and that's what many of us do with our teaching. No drinking! No dancing! No swearing! No sex!

Yet, Jesus specifically didn't teach like that. In fact, in Matthew 11:30, he point-blank says, "For my yoke is easy and my burden is light." The term *yoke* referred to a rabbi's interpretation of the Old Testament Law, as well as the extra-biblical expectations that were required of the rabbi's followers.

> The developing rabbinic tradition understood discipleship to entail learning from Pharisaic authorities and carrying out scrupulous observance of the oral law. Because the oral law was considered to be of divine origin, its massive obligations became far more burdensome than Scripture itself, and with the passing of years and the addition of more and more prescriptions, the rabbis could not lessen the burden without overthrowing the whole system.[11]

And that's exactly what Jesus did! He steps in and does what the religious leaders weren't willing to do. He goes in a completely different direction, calling his set of rules "easy" and "light." When Jesus is actually pushed by the religious leaders to talk about the important laws he was teaching his followers, he narrows it down to two: "'Love the Lord your God with all your heart and with all your soul and with all your mind.' This is the first and greatest commandment. And the second is like it: 'Love your neighbor as yourself.' All the Law and the Prophets hang on these two commandments" (Matt. 22:37-40).

This is pretty interesting, given what we previously discovered concerning the whole point of teaching, huh? Jesus' commands all boil down to *love*: Love God with everything you've got, and love others *the way you love yourself*. This all goes back to a person's identity and what she believes about herself.

IDENTITY FORMATION

According to clinical and developmental psychologist James Marcia, every adolescent needs two crucial things during the teenage years for healthy identity formation: exploration and commitment. He even writes that one of the two most critical areas where this is true is in our ideology (i.e., the beliefs and doctrines that guide everything we do).[12] Without healthy exploration of our beliefs and doctrines, we can't have a real commitment to them. Instead, it's just a regurgitation of information or acting in a way we *think* we're supposed to act in a given moment.

Every youth worker has stories about a student they prayed with to accept Christ during an outreach event, retreat, or camp who within weeks or months was living no differently than before. Most of the time the reason this happens is because these students committed to something they never really explored and tested, which makes the decision shallow and impulsive. In too many of our churches, we focus heavily on the commitment aspect with prayers of salvation, altar calls, and attendance in church programs; but, consciously or unconsciously, we ignore (and at times even discourage) exploration of faith and theology. (We'll explore why this is the case in chapter 5, but for now we need to understand the damage it causes.)

Take a moment and think about your own personal faith: What has led to growth in your relationship with Jesus and your beliefs over the years? What originally drew you to Jesus in the first place?

Every time I ask these questions and think about my own responses, the answer to both is always the same: experiences. And more often than not, these experiences are of suffering and pain, not just experiences of joy.

It's in these situations of suffering that our hearts break. Nothing makes sense anymore. Dreams disappear like smoke and seem impossibly out of reach. We lose control. We lose our faith. Doubt creeps in and other people's prosperity seems to taunt us rather than cause us joy. Then we try really, desperately hard to get things back on track. We work and stress and plot...*we explore* everything we possibly can to find hope and a better understanding of who we are, who God is, and what the point of living really is.

From my own faith story, it was being bullied throughout elementary school that made me question if I was loved and had any worth.

It was the repeated trauma that occurred during just a couple of months in middle school when my grandmother passed away, a kid on my little league team died after a battle with leukemia, and I was buried alive by snow falling off my roof while I was building a snow fort[13] that made me ask my parents questions about mortality and the afterlife.

It was not getting into college the first time I applied that made me rethink my future and purpose.

It was all of those books, Bible professors, sermons, mission trips, and conversations with people that poked holes in my theology and understanding of God, subsequently creating a crisis of faith that made me refine my beliefs and go deeper than what I'd previously thought to be true.

It was driving myself into the ground emotionally, physically, and spiritually during my first year of marriage in order to work a part-time paid church position, along with two other jobs, that made me reconsider what calling meant.

It was forcing my wife to work a job she hated just so we could pay the bills, and then having our first year of marriage almost end in divorce that made me reconsider what a godly marriage looks like.

And most recently, it was five years of struggling with infertility, a miscarriage, and a two-year endeavor with our state's foster care system to adopt our son.[14] And then in the middle of that whole process, my wife miraculously got pregnant with our daughter (who is only 17 months younger than our son). That whole experience taught and challenged my faith in so many ways that I could write a whole other book on just that!

I know you could write your list too. *And so can your teenagers.* The fact of the matter is that being pushed to explore the validity of what we believe is guaranteed in life, and it's guaranteed to happen over and over and over again as God redeems our experiences to bring us to a deeper and more mature faith in him.[15]

One of my adjunct college professors used to tell our class that the main goal of youth ministry is to purposefully create a crisis of faith for our teenagers and then help them explore possible solutions. As Lem Usita, a youth ministry professor at San Diego Christian College, discussed during his talk on identity formation at The Youth Cartel's Summit in 2013, the problem is we don't do this very well. It's one of the reasons many of our teens are walking away from the faith after they graduate from high school. Sadly, college is one of the first times when many Christian students are given a chance to explore their faith, as compared to their earlier religious settings where they were told what to believe. As our teens are met with deeper thinking, new ideas, and challenges they haven't encountered before, they reconsider what their parents, church, and youth workers told them to believe. In the process, they disappear from church because—consciously or unconsciously—they feel like the church doesn't allow for questions and exploring.

HOW WE AVOID EXPLORATION

In our culture, teenagers are surrounded by and taught all the "correct" answers they need for life. At school they learn how to digest the information they need for a quiz or test, but they never allow the information to reach their hearts for deeper, lifelong understanding. Often, the information is quickly forgotten once the test is out of the way. Unfortunately, this way of learning hasn't stayed in the classroom but has crept into the church as well.

I'm sure you've heard the story about the children's sermon where a pastor describes a squirrel with an acorn in a tree. And when he's finished, he asks the kids to name what he just described. Their answer is (all together now)..."JEEEESUS!" Unfortunately, our teens aren't too far off from this scenario. When asked questions about the Bible or their faith, most are able to give surface-level answers, but many would be hard-pressed to explain their answers more deeply or provide a Scripture reference to support them.

On top of that, one of the other things we need to understand about a post-Christian environment and how it impacts the teens we interact with, especially those who don't have a church background, is that the act of exploring multiple opinions and worldviews is in full bloom. It seems like more and more, I'm engaging with teens who don't have much Bible knowledge but know all about Darwinian evolution, Buddhist meditation, the idea of karma, interactions with the spirit world through psychics, and other beliefs and ideas from outside Judeo-

Christian tradition.

With full access to the Internet 24 hours a day, teenagers have a portal to worlds of information about various religions, and most are encouraged to explore their personal beliefs in almost every avenue of their lives. However, in this post-Christian era, many public schools are hypervigilant in their efforts *not* to push Christianity, and I've known a lot of teenagers who've felt like they were free to talk about every belief system at their school *except* ours. Discussions in history, science, or even English classes might touch on ideas from Buddhism, Islam, Darwin, or Judaism. But some teenagers feel that if they try to throw the Bible into these conversations, they'll be shut down. (And some of them have been.)

The big question we need to ask about our teaching in our churches is how we handle teens who ask questions because of something they read, heard, or saw that challenges what we've previously taught them or would normally teach them. There are three disservices we do to our teenagers that can damage their beneficial faith exploration:

1. Telling them the correct answer.

As Christy Lang shared during her talk "Changing Focus: Reading the Bible with Youth" at The Youth Cartel Summit in 2013, we need to face the reality that most of our teenagers today are bored with the Bible and there is a huge decline in biblical literacy rates among teens.[16] Most teens, and many adults as well, approach the Bible as if it belongs to someone else. It's almost like they approach it as a vitamin—something they passively take in. More so, Lang shared that most people expect someone else—a trained pastor, church leader, Bible study leader, youth group volunteer, etc.—to be the one who takes the responsibility to give them that "vitamin" and explain the Bible to them.

Think about it for a second: how many times have you had a teenager come off a retreat or mission trip with the goal of reading through the Bible? Now think about what the end result usually is for many of those teens. If your students are like mine, most of them give up somewhere around Leviticus. *Maybe* they make it to Numbers or Deuteronomy. But the fact is a lot of people easily grow confused with the Bible, feel like what they're reading isn't relevant to everyday life, and don't know how to think critically about the Scriptures and what they believe. So they give up and walk away.

Because we adults tend to tell teenagers what to believe instead of helping them engage the Scriptures on their own, our teens don't even begin to know how to explore the Bible more deeply. This is especially damaging when they graduate and aren't around us anymore. When their source for information about God disappears, so does any semblance of their faith.

2. Telling them, directly or indirectly, that questions are not okay.

How do you handle the teenager who tells you he's been reading the Quran lately?

Or how about the teen who admits to you that she thinks she

might be gay?

Or the kid who tells you that the more he thinks about it, the more he feels like Noah and the flood never really happened?

It seems to me that too many of us in the church just cut off the conversation, or even the relationship, rather than diving into a great conversation by asking questions and helping them explore what is going on inside of them. Somewhere along the line, we've bought into the myth that certain questions are not okay to ask, so we avoid them altogether.

It's also unfortunate that oftentimes, when we aren't just telling teenagers what the correct answers are in regard to hot topics like sexuality, abortion, or politics, we're actually giving the impression that these are topics the church doesn't discuss—despite the fact that *every other area* of life discusses topics like these openly. In essence, we're telling people that establishing a biblical worldview on these topics isn't worth their time. And then Christians get all up in arms about media and how Hollywood distorts what the Bible has to say about these topics. Honestly, it's time to stop whining and start realizing that we as the Church gave up our biblical authority on these issues by refusing to talk about them in the first place.

And again, the root of so many of these questions is really about teenagers' identities and their answers to the question "Who am I?" So when we cut off their questions and doubts, we're actually communicating to teens that they don't matter.

I love what Brock Morgan writes in *Youth Ministry in a Post-Christian World*:

> We should create an atmosphere where students feel free to express who they are in the moment and what they believe this afternoon—even if it's all going to be different tomorrow. In the midst of the adolescent roller coaster ride, the grace we give them might be one of the only places where they'll find it.[17]

3. Teaching them the Bible is the exclusive source of truth. Now, before you throw this book out the window and give me a one-star review on Amazon and claim that I'm heretical, let me explain.

I fully and unapologetically believe the Bible is the full Word of God and that, as Paul tells Timothy, "All Scripture is God-breathed and is useful for teaching, rebuking, correcting and training in righteousness, so that the servant of God may be thoroughly equipped for every good work" (2 Tim. 3:16-17). I also believe the Scriptures give us the fullest, clearest, and most direct view of truth—and that truth is absolute.

But (and I know it's a *big* but) truth is not *exclusive* to the Bible. Saying it a slightly different way: There is absolute truth, but it doesn't make everything else absolutely wrong.

In some way, shape, or form, I'd argue that most religions have areas of overlap with Christian teachings that we can affirm and agree upon. Again, I'm not saying we agree about everything, but there are glimpses of truth in lots of other worldviews. The problem we run into when we present this idea that truth is exclusive to the Bible is we're giving teens the message that they *always* have to pick and choose. One of the best examples of this is the debate over creation.

In his book *Already Gone*, Ken Ham (along with Britt Beemer and Todd Hillard) says one of the reasons so many young adults walk away from the faith is because the church has failed to teach a creationist view of Genesis 1 and 2.[18] The argument goes that if teenagers are allowed to question the foundation of how the world was created, they will carry that doubt over to their view of the Bible as a whole. Honestly, I couldn't disagree with their premise more. In fact, I think their ultra-narrow view is actually the larger reason why students want nothing to do with the church.

By arguing that the Bible is the exclusive source for an explanation on how the world was created, we're telling teens that science must be wrong. We pin them in a corner and tell them they have to pick one or the other. And the fact is, more and more teens are picking science because of the overwhelming evidence and data. But by being more open about exploring the possibilities of exactly how the world was created, we can change the conversation from a question of God versus science to a question of how God did it. Do you see the big difference there? As long as teenagers grasp the "God created" aspect of where everything came from, does it even matter *how* God did it?

I've come to the conclusion that it's far more important for a teen to own her beliefs and be able to intellectually articulate and defend them—even if those beliefs contradict what we've taught her. It's better that a teenager's beliefs are his own and not just a regurgitation of what we, his parents, or others in the church have told him he should believe. We need to come alongside our teens and help them explore what they really believe, because they're going to do it anyway—with or without us. It's time we start creating environments where questions and different opinions are welcomed and met with tolerance and loving challenge.

WHAT DOES EXPLORATION LOOK LIKE? CHAPTER 4

Since coming to each of the conclusions we've explored thus far in the book, I've tried numerous things in my teaching to better connect with a post-Christian culture, while at the same time helping my students encounter Jesus and explore what they really believe. Some of my attempts have fallen flat, and some have worked extremely well. There have also been a whole lot of things that work sometimes but don't work at other times. Hopefully my learning experiences will spare you some of the swings and misses I've had and help you create an environment where teens can explore their faith in a healthy and productive way.[19]

Before I go much further, though, I want to clarify one thought. For some, it would be very easy to take the practical ideas in this chapter and apply them only to small-group meetings. However, I've come to believe that changing the way we teach can be done in small groups and large groups alike. Regardless of our setting, it's crucial to teach in a way that helps teenagers explore their faith. So as you read this chapter, note that almost all of what I suggest can be done in any setting and with groups of any size.

Now let's dive in: What does exploration look like and what are some practical ways to create environments of exploration in our churches?

PREPPING FOR YOUR MEETING

Before we do anything else, the first and most important element of our teaching that we need to evaluate is ourselves. Are you open to exploring? If you're not willing to continue educating, challenging, and exploring your own beliefs, you might as well just put down this book and stop reading.

It doesn't matter how old you are, how much faith experience you have, or how many degrees you've earned. Albert Einstein famously said, "Intellectual growth should commence at birth and cease only at death." And it's this mind-set that will lay the entire foundation for whether or not your environment is one in which teens or young adults will be able to explore their faith. Honestly, creating an environment of exploration isn't something you can just focus on for an hour and a half during your Sunday school meeting or your Wednesday night youth meeting. It has to be a lifestyle and a posture of faith you live all week long.

One of the things that will need to change is how you prepare each week. For starters, this is all about what you're reading and studying. This means instead of picking up authors, commentaries, blogs, websites, videos, etc., that will simply back up what you already believe about a passage or topic, you're going to purposefully engage with sources from multiple perspectives that challenge what you've been taught and provide different ideas to consider. Unfortunately, this is probably going to add to your necessary prep time, but it's so important. It will help you present a topic or passage from a broader perspective, which we'll talk about more in a moment. But it will also help you be prepared for the multiple viewpoints that are likely to come up as your youth group interacts.

Beyond your study time and the resources you use on your own, it's also important to consider how you can include other people in your prep time. My senior pastor does a great job with this each week, taking the topic or passage he's teaching on and asking as many people as he can what they think about it. He does this in our staff meetings, at the YMCA during basketball games, and during one-on-ones throughout the week with others he's connecting with. This is something I've tried to mimic as well. I use my weekly student leadership meeting as part Bible study to go through the upcoming week's topic or text. Then the overall goal is to do as much listening as I can during the week. The multiple viewpoints and opinions you gather when you prepare this way can help you process the passage more fully; enable you to gauge where your group, congregation, or community is at with the given topic; and help the people you ask start exploring the topic prior to your meeting.

As you prepare, know that your illustrations and analogies for any given topic or passage will usually go further with today's young people if you're pulling from the wider culture around you and not just from Christian tradition. In an increasingly post-Christian world, these kinds of redemptive analogies are invaluable to communicating truth and Good News, especially with teenagers.

We have to understand that a majority of the young people in our youth groups are already watching, listening to, and talking about pop culture. It seems to me that too many pastors and youth workers spend their time trying to replace popular culture with Christian ripoffs (that are rarely as good, frankly), rather than simply using pop culture references as a springboard for deeper conversations. What's more, when we engage our churches with such widely relatable analogies, we're immediately equipping others to have relevant conversations about faith with non-Christian friends at school or work during the week.

It's for this reason that I'm *much* more excited about a movie like *Noah* than I am about a movie like *God's Not Dead*.[20] It will be a lot easier for me to gather a group of non-Christian teens to go see *Noah* than *God's Not Dead*. The Christian movie is often going to have a corny factor to it right off the bat, which shuts down most teens' openness to dialogue and conversations about faith.[21] And even if the *Noah* movie is way off base as far as the biblical account, who cares? If going to see that movie generates deeper conversations about the Bible, Noah's story, and the truth about Jesus, then isn't that the whole point?[22] (See chapter 2 for a refresher on why we teach.)

There is no better example of this than when Paul taught the Athenians about Jesus at Mars Hill (Acts 17:22-34). Rather than wasting his time in the Areopagus and telling the people why they are heathens and shouldn't be reading or participating in certain rituals, Paul uses Greek poetry and philosophy, along with a pagan altar with an inscription that says TO AN UNKNOWN

GOD, in order to share the message of Jesus with them. And he does it all while surrounded by penis-shaped stone idols. (Now *there's* a teaching outline to try at your next youth meeting!) The fact of the matter is, when we use examples from the wider, so-called "secular" culture, we will not only be meeting people where they're at, but we'll be helping equip those we're teaching with relevant ways to engage others and shine God's light outside our church doors.

Just to be clear, please don't ignore what I'm saying and hear instead what I'm *not* saying. I'm not saying all forms of art and literature from a secular standpoint have worth or entertainment value. I'm also *not* saying we should completely immerse ourselves in the world by watching and listening to everything we possibly can under the auspices of "ministry." Paul Borthwick, a professor and mentor of mine in college, joked that once you've seen one Madonna music video, you probably don't need to watch them all. And that's still true today for any artists pushing the boundaries of sexuality and other potentially offensive material.

What I *am* saying is that because truth is not exclusive to the Bible, why don't we take the things that the majority of people are consuming for entertainment, and use them to help people see the bits and pieces (heck, sometimes *boulders*) of truth that are already there? Sometimes I feel we as the church are handcuffing ourselves evangelistically. We're so concerned with protecting ourselves from the world that we forget we're actually supposed to be *in* it.

Another element of preparation you should become more

purposeful about is engaging the multiple learning styles that are present in your meetings. According to Neil D. Fleming, the developer of VARK learning styles, there are four different ways people learn:[23]

1. **V**isually. Visual learners are all about seeing the lesson being taught. The more images, charts, diagrams, videos, etc., the better.
2. **A**udibly. Audible learners are all about hearing the lesson. Stories, explanations, and lectures help them learn.
3. **R**eading and Writing. These learners are all about the printed word. They want to read the information for themselves and take notes about what they are processing.
4. **K**inesthetically or Tactically. This learning style is all about experiencing what is being taught. These learners want to feel, smell, taste, touch, and be hands-on as much as possible.

According to Fleming's research, we're fairly evenly divided when it comes to learning styles. In a May 2013 survey, reading and writing had a slight lead as the survey responders' primary learning style, coming in at 27.6 percent. Right behind it was kinesthetic learning at 27.2 percent. Audible learning came next at 24.4 percent, followed by visual learners at 20.8 percent.[24] On top of looking at which learning style was dominant for an individual, Fleming's research also suggests the majority of the population (64 percent) learns best when being engaged by more than one of these learning styles. [25]

What's important to understand from this research is that for most churches and ministries, we've largely depended on an audible style of teaching, especially on Sunday morning in our church services. This means we're regularly engaging only a quarter of our audience, at best, during our meetings. So, when you ask a week later for someone to recap what was discussed during the last youth group meeting, there are typically only a couple of students who respond, if any, right? If we truly want our students and listeners to explore their faith in a deeper way, we have to do a better job of engaging the different learning styles in our audience.

Here are a number of ways you can gear your youth meetings to engage each of these VARK learning styles. (What's great is that many of these will appeal to more than one learning style.)

VISUAL LEARNERS

- Look for images and pictures. (In other words, if you're looking at 2 Corinthians 6:14 and the idea of being unequally yoked, find a picture of yoked bulls to show while you explain it.)
- Look for movie clips or YouTube videos. (Hint: *Sermonspice.com* is a great resource to use.)
- Use an iPad app like Jot! to draw pictures or diagrams during your meeting.
- Think about what you could wear to help bring out the teaching. (If you're talking about homelessness, dress the part.)
- Use a website like *PollEverywhere.com* to do text

message polls with your students and see the survey results instantaneously.

AUDIBLE LEARNERS

• Come up with rhymes, songs, or acronyms to illustrate a point.

• Purchase an audio Bible and play it during your meeting to read the passage you're looking at.

• Ask others to share during part of the lesson, providing a couple of different voices as opposed to just your own. This could mean having someone share something God is doing in his or her life that connects to your topic. Or it could simply be having someone explain part of a text. (For example, while looking at James 3 and discussing what it means to tame the tongue, instead of you explaining what a bit in a horse's mouth is, ask someone from the group who rides horses to stand up and explain it.)

• Break into small groups to discuss a question or idea.

READING AND WRITING LEARNERS

• Make sure your teenagers have access to Bibles during your meeting or print copies of the passage so the group can look at it together.

• Write notes on a whiteboard during the meeting. (Better yet, ask a student to take notes.)

• Put together an outline that students can use to take notes or fill in the blanks as the meeting progresses.

• Write up some journaling questions and give them to the youth after the meeting. Encourage them to spend time answering them during the week.

KINESTHETIC LEARNERS

• Come up with object lessons that involve your group in part or as a whole to help illustrate the chosen passage.
• Allow your group to ask questions in the middle of the meeting either via text message or out loud.
• Plan your lesson as a debate and have your group take sides while they participate in discussing a certain topic or biblical text where two different viewpoints are common.
• Break up into small groups during the message and have them build or make something to go along with what you're discussing.

Obviously, these lists aren't exclusive in any way, shape, or form. If we truly want to help people explore their beliefs, then the challenge for all of us as teachers should be to try to be as creative and engaging as possible.

The last thing I want to encourage you to do for your midweek preparation is put together a prayer team (if you don't have one already). It's ultimately the job of the Holy Spirit to bring about change, clarity, and conviction, so a prayer team of three to five people lifting up your group is one of the most powerful tools I can recommend. (It's also a great way to get more people in your church, who may not have the time or desire to attend meetings and work hands-on with teens, involved with your youth ministry.)

Once you have a team, simply send out an email each week with a brief recap of what happened the previous week, a description of the topic you'll be discussing in the coming week, along with some specific prayer requests concerning your group's dynamics or even specific students.

DURING YOUR MEETING

From a practical standpoint, helping students explore means rethinking your role as a *teacher* and looking at yourself as a *facilitator* instead. Believe me, it's hard to stay in that role, especially for those who are gifted teachers. (I still struggle with doing this myself!)

Here are a number of practical ways to become a facilitator:

First, learn how to be part of a conversation. During your meetings ask a lot of questions and do as much as you can to get your group to discuss and talk as much as possible. When someone asks a good question, resist the urge to just dive in and answer it. Instead, use that question to help the whole group think deeper by pulling a Jesus and responding with a question. I also love turning the question back to the group by saying, "Great question! What does everyone else think?" Don't just do this during a small group or youth group meeting; find creative ways to do this in large groups as well.

I've started putting wireless microphones out among the crowd during our youth service. When I'm teaching up front, I encourage students to interrupt and ask questions, or to actually answer the questions I throw out. It makes the teaching time longer, but it's worth it.

By facilitating and being a part of the group, and not just teaching, you will not only help teenagers feel important and meaningful to the group, but you will also be surprised about what you learn about God, faith, and the Bible. Honestly, every time I use this format rather than just teaching, I have my list of things that I want to make sure get put out there for the youth to consider. Yet, I rarely have to share those things myself because my students bring up every point in a more natural way during the group discussion.

Now, that being said, this *does not mean* there is never a time to teach or explain something. There will be times when, as the person who's taken the time to study the topic beforehand, you will need to explain the background of a passage you're discussing. Or there will be times when you will ask a question and be met with silence. When that happens, it's completely okay to jump in and provide some thoughts to your own question. I highly recommend sharing a couple answers you've heard in response to the question you just asked, and then turn it back to the youth and ask what they think. This is a big reason why it's important that you fully explore the topic or passage yourself. Sharing a handful of ways some people may look at a passage or topic will go much further in helping your teens think critically about their beliefs.

Another great way to handle a silent room is to prep volunteers beforehand and let one of them jump in and respond. That way you're encouraging participation from multiple people, and it maintains a conversational feel. Then you can ask the group if they agree or disagree with that person's response, and also ask them to explain why.

Second, make sure multiple people get the opportunity to share. As you facilitate conversations, you'll most likely encounter certain people who tend to dominate the dialogue or are always the first ones to grab the microphone when you ask a question. (You probably had a person or two come to mind as you read that last sentence.) To avoid this scenario, an easy solution is to pose questions directly to those people in the group who haven't shared yet. However, it's important to let everyone know up front that they don't have to share or that "I don't know" is a perfectly valid answer. Many times when you get a noncommittal response like that, there's a good chance the person is simply processing the information being shared.

Third, make it your goal to challenge the typical answers. When you're talking about a subject, don't just present your church's "correct" theological answer. Instead, do your best to stay neutral in how you present the information. When someone shares an opinion, your best tool is going to be the question "Why?" Learn to play the devil's advocate and challenge them to defend what they're sharing. Ask them to explain their answers and back up their statements. By doing this, you'll help teenagers really think about what they're saying and what they believe.

Fourth, avoid using overtly Christian language.[26] For those coming out of a post-Christian context who have little to no church background, words like *sin*, *grace*, *justification*, *salvation*, *saved*, and the like have a good chance of going over their heads. Or worse, students might have an inaccurate definition of such terms and completely misunderstand what you intended to communicate. The words we use to communicate about Jesus are really important, and just because a word is found in the Bible or used by theologians that doesn't mean we're required to use it. We can say the exact same things while using more relevant terms, and it will help people avoid confusion and actually understand what's being said. Personally, when I use any theological terms during a youth meeting, I immediately explain the word in a couple different ways or ask someone from the group to define it (usually the best option).

Fifth, seek to have group discussions that are organic and unstructured—the more you can let them evolve on their own, the better. The goal of each of your meetings shouldn't be to get through all of the materials you've prepared. Instead, as you facilitate conversations, you must learn to jump around based on what topics your group is bringing up, rather than following your specific outline. Also, if you need to end one week with "to be continued," that's totally fine. Sometimes having your conversation over the span of two or three weeks will do the topic more justice and make it more engaging. There is nothing better for an exploratory environment than when people leave feeling excited to come back the next week and continue the conversation. Often, you'll find that some teens in your group will do some homework and study the topic further on their own in between meetings, which is exactly what you want!

Sixth, leave people hanging. I realize this is probably the most difficult thing you'll have to do. But when the conversation is nearing an end, resist the urge to reveal which answer is the "right" one and instead challenge everyone to keep wrestling with the issue.

Once again, please don't hear what I'm *not* saying. I'm *not* saying you should never take a theological stand from your perspective or never share your opinion. I *am* arguing that our goal should be to help our students think through their own beliefs, and sometimes one of the best ways to do that is by hearing different opinions, including yours. However, I've found it better not to share my perspective until someone specifically asks for it. And even then, sometimes I tell my students that I'll tell them what I think later on in a one-on-one or small-group setting. The reason I do that is because too often when a pastor or ministry leader shares his or her opinion, the conversation and thinking in the group tends to stop. Sometimes it's because of *how* we share it, but sometimes it's just because the teenagers assume the answer has been found and there's no more work to do. (This does such a disservice to our students.)

When sharing our opinion isn't our primary mode of teaching, what we think about a given topic still tends to flow naturally into the conversation, which gives space for teens to process—as well as question—the perspective we're offering.

AFTER YOUR MEETING

One of the biggest things we need to do more of is give our teens the tools and resources to continue wrestling with faith on their own. Harkening back to Christy Lang's comments about how teens approach the Bible, we can't just spoon-feed everyone his or her faith all the time. We have to teach people how to dig into their beliefs on their own.

For starters, this means making sure your group has Scripture references, suggested articles, websites, podcasts, and other resources in hand as they leave your meetings. Only a handful will leave knowing where to look for more information on their own. The others need to be led to those things. This can be done on a PowerPoint slide at the end of your teaching time, with options for people to write them down so they can check them out at home. Or you might hand out a preprinted postcard that lists ideas for how to go deeper. It might mean creating Facebook or Twitter posts throughout the week. Or maybe it means challenging your group to ask certain questions of their classmates, coworkers, etc., during the week—what many call a "listening tour" on the topic discussed.

Beyond getting content into people's hands, we also need to proactively teach them how to engage that content, specifically the Bible. Gone are the days when the information you need to accurately exegete a Bible passage can be found only in a seminary and senior pastors' libraries. Thanks to the Internet and sites like *BibleGateway.com* (as well as apps like Olive Tree or Blue Letter Bible), it's pretty easy to access a wealth of information to help us understand Scripture. We need to teach people how to use the tools available to them, such as commentaries, concordances, and Greek/Hebrew dictionaries, so they can use their intellect when it comes to the Bible and not just their feelings or experiences.

The problem is, a post-Christian context reverses the role of these things when it comes to defining what is right and true. Experiences, feelings, and opinions are put on a pedestal and given worth first and foremost—even when they may contradict the actual meaning. In light of this reactionary approach to Scripture, it's important to remind teens that the Bible can't mean something now that it *didn't* mean at the time it was written. So once we understand the original meaning of a Bible verse, we can translate the message into our everyday lives—which is a simple way of describing hermeneutics. [27]

Lastly, as our job shifts more toward creating conversations, we have to remember that these conversations aren't supposed to last for only an hour at church or in youth group, but they should be ongoing throughout the week. It's important to find ways to help people continue to comment, share, and discuss what they are processing all week long. For many churches, the easy way to do this is by utilizing small groups during the week, where people can come together to debate and voice their thoughts. This could mean being really proactive on social media to create conversation threads, or it could mean having actual dialogue in coffee shops and during football games. Simply make sure that you—along with the other leaders or volunteers—are actively seeking out ways to talk to others throughout the week.

As you can tell, creating environments that help people explore their beliefs takes a bit more work than we may be accustomed to. But I promise you that when we pull these things off, even in part, it's worth it to see young people make their faith and their relationships with Jesus more and more personal.

CHAPTER 5

Rob Bell is by far my favorite author and speaker. Without fail, everything he writes or produces I try to get ahold of as fast as I can. I think I preordered his book *What We Talk About When We Talk About God* as early as humanly possible.[28] My iTunes library is full of his sermons from Mars Hill Bible Church in Michigan, and my students at church often joke with me about my "man crush" on Rob.

Honestly though, I'm almost reluctant to admit any of this since his book *Love Wins* came out in 2011.[29] My wife and I don't like to mention him in a Facebook status because we're afraid of the backlash we may get from our more conservative friends or church members. In fact, when I share something he wrote or said while I'm teaching or talking to other pastors or youth workers, I usually leave him nameless, referring to him vaguely as "an author," "a pastor," or "a blogger," just to avoid pushback and criticism.[30]

But here's the thing, the reason I love his content so much is because he makes me think—even when I don't agree 100 percent with everything he says. He is *not* Jesus, and he is not infallible. But he is a brilliant communicator who asks fantastic questions that challenge the status quo, forcing people to dig below the surface of what they really believe or think. It's for this reason that I loved *Love Wins* and personally think Christendom's general response to it, labeling him a heretic, was pathetic—particularly when some of the ones doing the labeling never even read the book.

The intense reaction seemed to be rooted in this pervasive attitude that any kind of exploration within our faith is dangerous. But why is this so often the case in the Church? Why are we so concerned about one pastor asking some big questions that our response is to write a bunch of Facebook updates, blog posts, or even books to make sure everyone knows the questions being asked have already been 100 percent answered and shouldn't be asked again ever?[31] As mentioned in chapter 2, why are we so focused on getting people to commit to Jesus, while in many cases we also discourage and ignore those who want to *explore* their faith?

As I've wrestled with questions like this throughout my own ministry, I've come up with six answers:

1. We discourage exploration because we confuse a lack of faith with doubt.

For some Christians, the aspect of asking questions and doubting is opening up a possible floodgate that ends with someone rejecting Jesus and Christianity altogether. Thus is the conclusion of Ken Ham concerning the creation account: If someone doubts Genesis 1 and 2, it could lead them to doubt Genesis 3 and every other chapter in the Bible. As Holly Rankin Zaher pointed out during her talk at The Youth Cartel Summit in 2013, "Christians have at some point picked up the idea that doubt is the *opposite* of faith and is a bad thing."

Chances are that since you're reading this book, you're some kind of pastor or church leader. Despite your position within church leadership, I'd bet that at some point in your walk with

Jesus, you've had doubts about your faith, God, and the Bible. And if you're really honest, there is probably at least one aspect of your faith that you're doubting or wrestling with right now. Chances are also pretty high that you wouldn't even think about mentioning that doubt to a soul—especially not within your own church, lest you be disqualified from ministry.

Here's the thing, though: doubt is not the opposite of faith. And as Rankin Zaher pointed out, "The true opposite of faith is certainty. If we're certain about everything, *we don't need faith*."

Throughout Jesus' ministry, the two groups that were always in direct opposition to him were the Pharisees and the Sadducees, the religious leaders of the time. The number one point of contention was the insistence that these religious leaders didn't need Jesus, grace, or faith. They had everything figured out, and they knew all the answers. They'd spent years studying the Jewish Scriptures, debating what they actually believed, and then developing the perfect religion to ensure they were living a pious life and honoring God. There wasn't one ounce of space for doubting anything they knew, and that resulted in their looking the Messiah directly in the face and walking the other way.

In contrast, I'd argue that the exact opposite motivation was at the core of the disciples who decided to follow Jesus. As he called these fishermen, tax collectors, and other men to follow him around and learn from him, one of their first thoughts had to be, *Hmmm, maybe there is something different than what we've been taught?* And isn't it the same for each of us? Before we decided to follow Christ, we had to start with the same exact question. The fact is, without doubt's continuous role in our lives, our faith would be shallow and empty.

I believe it's important that we understand the story of "Doubting Thomas" found in John 20:24-29.

> Now Thomas (also known as Didymus), one of the Twelve, was not with the disciples when Jesus came. So the other disciples told him, "We have seen the Lord!"
>
> But he said to them, "Unless I see the nail marks in his hands and put my finger where the nails were, and put my hand into his side, I will not believe."
>
> A week later his disciples were in the house again, and Thomas was with them. Though the doors were locked, Jesus came and stood among them and said, "Peace be with you!" Then he said to Thomas, "Put your finger here; see my hands. Reach out your hand and put it into my side. Stop doubting and believe."
>
> Thomas said to him, "My Lord and my God!"
>
> Then Jesus told him, "Because you have seen me, you have believed; blessed are those who have not seen and yet have believed."

For many, it seems like Thomas gets such a bad rap, as if the nickname "Doubter" is a negative attribute forever connected with his name. However, Jesus wasn't shy about calling out his disciples. More than once he told them they were fools and they had weak faith. But he doesn't do that here with Thomas. Instead, he shows up in person and he invites Thomas to explore—to touch the holes in his hands and put his hand in Jesus' side. If Jesus can do that with Thomas's doubts, then he can also do it with ours.

2. We discourage exploration because we're scared about what-ifs. Back in 2007, an atheist named Hemant Mehta decided to sell his soul on eBay to the highest bidder.[32] His offer was that for every $10 of the winning bid, he'd go to any church, mosque, or synagogue that the winning bidder chose. The result was a $504 winning bid that developed into Mehta visiting numerous churches across the country and publishing a very insightful and thought-provoking book about his experience called *I Sold My Soul on eBay*. Here's one of his conclusions from the book:

> Evangelical pastors I hear about in the media seem to perceive just about everything to be a threat against Christianity. Evolution is a threat. Gay marriage is a threat. A swear word uttered accidentally on television is a threat. Democrats are a threat. And so on.
>
> I don't see how any of these things pose a threat against Christianity. If someone disagrees with you about politics, or social issues, or the matter of origins, isn't that just democracy and free speech in action? How

do opposing viewpoints constitute a threat? The ideas that can be defended with reasoning or evidence will stand while others fall. But if all these issues are spun as if they are threats, [a conservative megachurch] has an army of thousands of people who are being told to be stubborn about their beliefs. Why do Christians feel so threatened?[33]

Let's face it, challenging teenagers to explore their faith can be terrifying. What if they don't come to the same conclusion I have and thus arrive at the "wrong" answer? What if a parent or church leader gets upset because their children go in a different direction than what they or their denomination believe? What if a teen decides to de-emphasize Scripture and instead places a higher priority on feelings, science, or something else?

Be forewarned: *All of those things will happen as you help teenagers explore their faith!* (They've all happened to me!) My favorite experience was when I was grilled by a parent for not sharing *my* opinion on what God thinks about tattoos (i.e., this mom assumed that, like her, I also believe tattoos are wrong, and she wanted me to tell the students that). She wasn't happy that I left the discussion hanging and challenged the youth to wrestle with the Bible and make their own decisions. And it really didn't help our conversation when I decided to share my true personal opinion with her—the one she wanted so badly—which was that tattoos are okay. (Needless to say, that family left our church shortly after that.)

The fact is, when we operate out of fear, it reveals a lack of trust in God. To be fearful of certain content and feel the need to control what someone hears or doesn't hear about God (in such specific ways) is basically like we're saying something is too big for God to handle.

After attending Rob Bell's *Love Wins* book release event in New York City, my wife had a dream that I think is a powerful example of the role fear should have in our faith. I'll let her describe it in her own words:

> After the talk, Rob asked if anyone wanted to go grab some food and continue discussing. I and one other guy volunteered. I jumped in the front seat of Rob's car with the other dude in the back. On our way there, we stopped in this giant parking lot. At the far end of the lot was a huge steel fence, and beyond that was a huge abyss—think Grand Canyon. We were all talking when all of a sudden Rob slams on the gas. The car jerks forward and we're racing at top speed toward the fence and the abyss beyond. I'm screaming, the dude in the back is screaming, and all the while Rob has a determined look on his face. We slam into the fence and stop in our tracks, all without any harm coming to us or to the car.
>
> I turn to Rob and scream at him, "Why did you do that?"
>
> Rob grins, throws his head back, and laughs. "Because I knew the fence would stop us," he says calmly.

To me, this dream signified that Rob isn't afraid to head full tilt toward the really hard questions because he has full confidence in the truth.

We don't have to live in fear when it comes to helping young people explore their faith, because it isn't our job to bring about change in our students. It's the Holy Spirit's job to do that. And he is capable of dealing with whatever we throw at him.We can push things into uncomfortable places knowing the Holy Spirit is at work in the lives of our teenagers and he is untimely in control of where they will land in regard to his truth.

Our job is to do everything we can to point students to Jesus and give them all the tools they need to operate within a relationship with Christ. The beauty of God's love for us is the gift of free will, and that means we have to allow our students to make authentic decisions about their beliefs, even when they might not be the same decisions we made.

3. We discourage exploration because we feel better about counting conversions.

Our church leaders love numbers as much as our culture does, and the number many church leaders love the most is our conversion rate. It's pretty easy to write and design a great talk, connect it with some worship, and turn up enough emotional heat to result in a great altar call. And it's exciting to sit and pray "the prayer" with students while we lead them in commitments to Christ. In fact, when I have the chance to do this, I walk away from youth group pumped up and feeling like I'm really accomplishing something.

However, as I already pointed out in chapter 3, the problem with this practice is that a true and lasting commitment can't exist without exploration. This means when a commitment to follow Christ is solely based on emotions, peer pressure, or anything else, it's going to be shallow and short-lived. That's not to suggest we should never have altar calls or challenge students to commit to Christ; it just means that such challenges must be balanced with space for critical thinking and deeper understanding.[34]

On top of this, we also forget that the journey toward Christ is just as important as the destination. Within a lot of churches we put a special emphasis on "sealing the deal." Yet studies will tell you that before a person makes a commitment to Christ, there are a number of touchpoints that have happened previously. Maybe you or your church aren't supposed to participate in a teen's final decision, and God is using you to plant some seeds that will blossom down the road instead. Again, when we focus so much on a conversion we can count, we forget that God is ultimately the one in control. As Paul shares in 1 Corinthians 3:6, "I planted the seed, Apollos watered it, but God has been making it grow."

Another problem we can run into when we emphasize the numbers to determine our effectiveness is that many of the teens aren't attending our programs all the time. So much of what we do with students is outside of our youth meetings: at Starbucks, at the high school, on the athletic field, in a classroom, or elsewhere. This makes it much harder to track and quantify what ministry is going on and how many teens we're impacting.

Beyond that, I've also found that when we really help a teenager explore his faith (and he eventually owns it), there is much more buy-in that leads to sharing that faith with others. This doesn't always mean an increase in our program numbers, but sometimes it does. Specifically, I've found that non-Christian students feel more comfortable coming to check things out in our youth group because they've been told they don't have to agree with us.

But for some of my other teens, it means increased conversations in the lunchroom; for another it meant starting an interfaith dialogue club at the high school. And honestly, I think things like that are even more effective in helping teens encounter Christ than doing everything we can to get our students to bring their friends to our programs so *we* can tell them about Christ.

4. We discourage exploration because we think students can't handle longer and more in-depth conversations.

All of us in youth ministry have read and heard over and over again about the limitations of teenagers—specifically middle schoolers—when it comes to the issue of their attention spans and what they can understand. It's been explained to me how middle schoolers can handle just a 10-to-15-minute talk (maximum) or else we'll lose them and bore them. A parent told me her eighth grade daughter wasn't "intellectually capable" of handling a talk in the 30-minute range. (Yes, her own parent said that.)

I've witnessed youth group leaders wrestle through a 15-minute talk because the youth kept talking and giggling and being disruptive. I've seen a small-group discussion fail miserably because all the teenagers wanted to do was go back to their game of *Call of Duty*.

On the other hand, I've also seen the exact opposite. I've watched a group of middle school students have such an engaging and deep conversation that parents began impatiently looking into the room when it went longer than the scheduled hour. I've watched teens take notes on a talk that lasted 45 minutes and then *continue* the conversation afterward. I've watched adolescents continue to respond to something God was doing within them once their camp speaker wrapped up his 50-minute sermon.

So, what's the appropriate length of time to engage teenagers, and why does it seem to work in one setting and not another? Based on my experiences, I've come to the conclusion that it isn't so much about our students and their developmental adolescent limitations. Instead, it has to do with how we treat them and what kind of environment we create.

Almost every time I've seen a leader struggle through a 15-minute talk, it's been in settings where the environment was built around games, entertainment, and a constant pleading with the youth to "just give 10 minutes of their time" to listen.

First, the idea of building the energy in a room and then expecting teens to settle down immediately for a talk is unrealistic. Our bodies simply aren't wired that way—especially not adolescent ones. Our bodies are wired to maintain their energy level and crash only once they're exhausted. This means that during our discussions, teens are either still flying high and bouncing off the walls, or they're falling asleep—neither of which is conducive for creating an environment in which they can explore their faith.

Second, I'd argue that by pleading with students to "just give me 10 minutes," we're unconsciously communicating to them that 10 minutes is all they can handle and they don't really want to hear what we have to say. So they're going to act accordingly. They may give us 10 minutes, but the message has already been communicated loud and clear that they're "just kids" with too much energy and ADHD. They end up barely making it through the talk because we unintentionally told them they would.

These are things we have to pay attention to because I think sometimes we set ourselves up (and our students) by creating an environment that tells them, "I know you can't really handle what I'm about to tell you, but I'm going to tell you anyway."

When students are engaged for longer periods of time, the environment has been set up the exact opposite of what I described above. Such thoughtfully programmed meetings may start with games, but they're designed to diminish gradually in energy, getting the teens to a point where they're calmer when it's time for the talk.

Also, there is no apology or plea made for the teens' time and attention. Instead, the speaker just dives in and goes for it. The students are treated like mature people with the capability to handle things bigger than themselves. And more often than not, I've watched teens rise to the occasion. They handle it for six or seven hours every day at school; why can't they handle it in our churches and ministries? Between creative teaching and treating them like the young adults they are (instead of like children who need to be handled with care), our teens can actually go much further than we think.

5. We discourage exploration because we like being the great teacher everyone comes to hear.

I love being up front and teaching teens, parents, or whoever will listen. A lot of that, I've come to learn, is simply my personality coupled with my gifting in teaching. Contrary to what some may think, it's okay to enjoy doing what we're good at. However, I'd be lying if I didn't admit that a small part—and honestly, sometimes it's a big part—of why I like teaching so much is my pride. It makes me feel good and important, while it feeds my sense of identity and worth.

When I first started wrestling with teaching my youth group differently, I knew it was going to mean that I had to share less and the teens had to share more. It meant I might not be the one to share a deep thought or cool analogy in a given week. Someone else's quote might get tweeted as opposed to something I said. There was a possibility that a teen would leave a meeting *not* thanking me, but instead thanking a peer for what she'd shared. My pride didn't like that.

Choosing to give in to our pride and ego, though, and allowing it to dictate how or why we teach teens distorts the entire process. First, it makes teaching a selfish act, which contradicts everything Christ modeled for us. Paul tells us in Philippians 2:3, "Do nothing out of selfish ambition or vain conceit. Rather, in humility value others above yourselves." Our job as teachers is to put the needs of others before our own and teach in a way that best helps them connect with Jesus. But this may not come naturally to every teacher, especially if it draws attention away from us.

Second, teaching for our own gain contradicts the message of Christ we're supposed to be sharing. As discussed, the whole goal of teaching is to help teenagers, parents, and anyone else who's listening understand that not only is their identity and worth rooted in Christ, his love for us, and the fact that he created us as his masterpieces, but also that there is *nothing* we can do to earn or lose that love. Yet, what does it say to teens when we do the exact opposite by calculating our worth and value based on what we do well (teach up front) and what affirmation we get from students or parents afterward?

Believe me, encouragement is fantastic and we all deserve it, especially as pastors and youth workers who are regularly bombarded with our fair share of criticisms. But there is a fine line between being encouraged by someone's words and looking for someone's words to define who we are. What would happen if your gift of speaking were taken away because of an injury that left you unable to speak? Are you less of a child of God because you can't teach anymore? No! Your gift of teaching doesn't dictate who you are; it's simply something you do out of your already established identity in Christ.

Last, when we let pride drive what we do and say, it can actually mute God's message altogether. What happens when God puts a message on our hearts that isn't fun for people to hear and won't result in personal praise? Part of helping people understand their identity in Christ means helping them understand why getting their identity from other things won't ultimately satisfy them. And people don't always want to hear that. Isn't this exactly what happened to Jesus?

Jesus knew his identity came from the Father, and he said the things that needed to be said. As much as people flocked to Jesus to see miracles and hear his amazing teaching, the Gospels also talk about the many people who walked away saying his teachings were too hard and they didn't want to trade their manmade worth for what God saw in them. If Jesus had been more concerned with what people were saying about him than he was about proclaiming God's message, his teachings would've been dramatically different, and they most certainly wouldn't have gotten him killed. (Which, you know, would've changed the entire course of human history as we know it.)

I hope you enjoy teaching, and I hope you find joy in living out the gifts God has given you. But if your hesitance toward some of the ideas in this book is solely about losing your role at the front of the room, you may have a bigger issue to deal with. If being up front is your motivation, then ministry *might* not be for you. As Paul said in Galatians 1:10, "Am I now trying to win the approval of human beings, or of God? Or am I trying to please people? If I were still trying to please people, I would not be a servant of Christ." Pointing people to Jesus needs to be our motivation in ministry because (God knows) pointing people to ourselves isn't going to get them very far.

6. We discourage exploration because telling everyone what to believe is easier.

Let's face it, doing things the way we've always done them is easier. It's more comfortable and faster to throw together our meetings the same way we've always done them and teach the same conclusions we've been teaching for years. It's easier if we don't have to survive that awkward moment when someone in the group responds to a discussion question with an answer that makes zero sense or is borderline offensive. It's quicker, neater, and cleaner to just preach or teach a 30-minute lesson, close in prayer, and let everyone go their own way. It's more comfortable for everyone when someone's emotional response to whatever is being discussed is limited to a personal email or voicemail later in the week, rather than being spilled out in front of everyone. It's much less stressful to teach in a way that doesn't rock the boat otherwise known as the elder board, parents, and the senior pastor.

I don't know about you, but when I read the Gospels, I feel like Jesus is constantly choosing the uphill route instead of what was easy:

Wouldn't it have been easier for Jesus to pick religious leaders to be his first disciples, since they already knew the Scriptures and the Jewish faith inside and out, rather than the Hebrew school dropouts he did choose?

Wouldn't it have been easier for Jesus to just wait until Sunday to heal people instead of doing it on the Sabbath and getting everyone worked up?

Wouldn't it have been easier for Jesus not to directly challenge the Pharisees and Sadducees and instead just silently let them do whatever they wanted to do?

Wouldn't it have been easier for Jesus to just teach love and goodness and sing "Kumbaya" and tell everyone to get along, rather than teaching tough things that made people walk away?

Wouldn't it have been easier for Jesus to live his life in a way that *didn't* get him killed for being a heretic?

I'm not saying that "easier" should never factor into any discussion within the church. What I *am* saying is that what's easiest is not always what's most effective. Change is difficult for many people—and it seems to be really difficult for most church communities. But we can't keep hitting the easy button just because it worked in the past. The fact is, many churches across the country are continuing to do what's easiest, and they're getting smaller and smaller every year. When this happens, we need to ask tough questions: *Do we care more about keeping our church nice and tidy and doing what we've always done for the sake of what's easy? Or do we care about reaching people for Jesus outside our church's walls?*

CHAPTER 6

I've wrestled deeply over the years with the fact that more and more high school graduates are walking away from the Church, and I've personally come to the conclusion that I think it's a good thing.

I think it's good that teenagers are encountering an environment—whether in college or the "real world"—that challenges their faith and makes them think through what they actually believe.

I think it's good that teenagers are making decisions for themselves and working through conflicting perspectives to reach their own conclusions.

And honestly, I think it's good that young adults are walking away from churches because by doing so, they are daring us as ministry leaders to give them a better picture of Jesus.

The fact is many young people aren't actually walking away from Jesus when they disappear from corporate Christianity. Dan Kimball makes this abundantly clear in his book *They Like Jesus but Not the Church.*[35] They are walking away from political agendas, fundamental views of the Bible, arrogant and negative thinking, and organized religion that has failed to prove its relevance in their everyday lives.

For most of us in church leadership, this negative impression of Christianity and the Church isn't something we set out to give people who were once in our spiritual care. It's usually just the consequence of unintentionally offering them a weak and unattractive version of faith. As youth workers in particular, we might have started out with a passion to help teens find Christ and grow into their identities in him, but maybe we've let our ministry become distracted with other things over the years.

John Ortberg describes this process well in the 2010 Spring Edition of *Leadership Journal*:

> Out of this vision [of who Christ is and what he wants to accomplish] flows a desire to do good things for such a God. And sometimes these activities may lead to results that look quite remarkable or impressive... [Eventually] people begin to pay more attention to what they are doing than to the reality of God.
>
> At this point the mission replaces the vision as the dominant feature in people's consciousness. Once this happens, descent is inevitable. For now people are living under the tyranny of Producing Impressive Results.[36]

And this is what teenagers leave our ministries with: a vision about Jesus that is all about "Producing Impressive Results." Some of our teens are given a vision that's all about having impressive theological answers that align with our denominations or deacon boards. Others are given a vision that's nothing more than an impressive list of dos and don'ts focused on how to live so we can be "good Christians." And still others leave with a vision of faith and the Church that's all about "bigger is better"—even if it means watering down the message we say we believe.

Is producing impressive results/theologies/behaviors in our ministries and teenagers a sin? No, not always. Everything mentioned above is good. However, when churches focus on these things as their top priorities instead of Christ, it's sinful. It's idolatry. And it's no wonder so many teenagers want nothing to do with the Church once they're gone. Sadly, many of us need to understand that the vision we're preaching and teaching in youth group and on Sunday morning is one that Jesus himself would walk away from too.

The direction God wants us to go is toward him. That's what the whole point of church is. Church should be a group of people who regularly gather in an effort to draw closer to God, live life together in love and service, and share God with others. That's it! There are no rules or guidelines about how that specifically looks, sounds, or feels. It's not about external elements, changing our behaviors first, or having all the answers. Instead, it's all about a group of people gathering together to live out the identity that was put within us from the beginning of time when God created us. It's about knowing how to love solely because we were first loved.

Today, there are very impressive churches meeting all around the world. You can walk into a beautiful building, hear incredible music and fantastic teaching, and participate in some amazing programs to help others in need—all while being surrounded by hundreds or thousands of others who are doing the same things. None of that really matters though. What matters is where the hearts of the leaders and members are focused.

Consider the letter to the church in Ephesus recorded in Revelation 2:2-3 (NLT):

> I know all the things you do. I have seen your hard work and your patient endurance. I know you don't tolerate evil people. You have examined the claims of those who say they are apostles but are not. You have discovered they are liars. You have patiently suffered for me without quitting.

Jesus is saying, "You are a good church doing many good things!" However, he then continues in verses 4 and 5 (emphasis mine):

> **But** [one of the most important words in Scripture] I have this complaint against you. You don't love me or each other as you did at first! Look how far you have fallen! Turn back to me and do the works you did at first. If you don't repent, I will come and remove your lampstand from its place among the churches.

This message is just as much for us today as it was for the church in Ephesus almost 2,000 years ago. As we serve and lead a local body of Christ's church, we cannot allow ourselves to make our gatherings focused on external things that can take the place of God within our hearts. Instead, we must stay focused on the love of Christ—his sacrifice, his resurrection, his grace, and the impact of those things on the hearts of those who come together.

My prayer is that we'd all teach in such a way that as our teens explore their faith—by asking questions and digging deeper through conversations with one another—they will passionately and unapologetically fall in love with Jesus and fully embrace their identity in him. And as we create communities where teenagers can come together from different backgrounds and differing opinions, my hope is that we can debate thoughtfully about the minors while still majoring on the major who is Jesus Christ. If we can do that, then *that* is a vision our teens will not only embrace, but also use to change the world.

SUGGESTED RESOURCES

Rob Bell, *Poets/Prophets/Preachers* (Grand Rapids, MI: Live Films, 2009) DVD

Kenda Creasy Dean, *Almost Christian* (New York: Oxford University Press, 2010)

John Dewey, *Experience and Education* (New York: Simon & Schuster, 1938)

Dan Kimball, *They Like Jesus but Not the Church* (Grand Rapids, MI: Zondervan, 2007)

David Kinnaman and Gabe Lyons, *UnChristian* (Grand Rapids, MI: Baker, 2007)

David Kinnaman, *You Lost Me* (Grand Rapids, MI: Baker, 2011)

Gabe Lyons, *The Next Christians* (Colorado Springs: Multnomah, 2012)

Hemant Mehta, *I Sold My Soul on eBay* (Colorado Springs: Waterbrook, 2007)

Brock Morgan, *Youth Ministry in a Post-Christian World* (San Diego: Youth Cartel, 2013)

Mark Oestreicher, *Youth Ministry 3.0* (Grand Rapids, MI; Zondervan/Youth Specialties, 2008)

Christian Smith and Melinda Lundquist Denton, *Soul Searching* (New York: Oxford University Press, 2005)

John Stott, *Between Two Worlds: The Challenge of Preaching in the Twentieth Century* (Grand Rapids, MI: Eerdmans, 1982)

ENDNOTES

[1] If the idea of a post-Christian culture is new to you, pick up a copy of *Youth Ministry in a Post-Christian World: A Hopeful Wake-Up Call* by Brock Morgan (The Youth Cartel, 2013).

[2] I did get an apologetic call from my friend later.

[3] Acts 1:15

[4] Frank E. Gaebelein, ed., *The Expositor's Bible Commentary: Matthew, Mark, Luke*, (Grand Rapids, MI: Zondervan, 1984).

[5] Rob Bell, "What is the Bible? Part 32: The Importance of Altitude," *Rob Bell* (blog), January 23, 2014, http://robbellcom.tumblr.com/post/74304654649/what-is-the-bible-part-32-the-importance-of-altitude.

[6] Michael Gungor and Lisa Gungor, "Cannot Keep You," *Beautiful Things* (Atlanta, GA: Brash Music, 2010).

[7] This has always been one of my favorite sayings from Mike Yaconelli.

[8] Steven Todd, "Post-Church Christians: A Journalist Explores the Implications of Believers Who Are Quitting Church," *YouthWorker Journal* (blog), February 10, 2009, www.youthworker.com/youth-ministry-resources-ideas/youth-ministry/11599465/.

[9] I'm not saying this to imply the sacrament of baptism shouldn't be practiced or isn't important, but I can't help but wonder if there was something more, something even deeper that Jesus was getting at—as was often the case.

[10] Again, remember in chapter 2 how we talked about this gospel message, along with *baptizo* and *onoma* in the Great Commission, implying that what we're really doing is sharing an encounter with Jesus that offers others the truth of who God is and their identity in him.

[11] Michael J. Wilkins, *Matthew*, NIV Application Commentary (Grand Rapids, MI: Zondervan, 2009), "An Invitation to the Weary and Burdened" (11:28-30).

[12] James E. Marcia, "Ego-Identity Status," *Social Encounters: Readings in Social Interaction*, Michael Argyle, ed. (New York, NY: Penguin, 1973), 340.

[13] I'm super thankful that my neighbor Pat was nearby, realized what had happened, and dug me out!

[14] If you're not familiar with foster care, our state requires a six-month process of training before you can get the necessary license to even have a chance at adopting a child. After we got the call and picked up a seven-day-old little boy, it was then a 13-month process of not knowing how his case would go or if we'd have to give him back to a rehabilitated birth mother (which would have been a good thing, right?). Once his birth parents were ruled out as caregivers, it was another five months before we were able to legally adopt him.

[15] Genesis 50:20; Romans 8:28; and James 1:2-4

[16] Yup, it's my second reference to material presented at The Youth Cartel's Summit. I want to assure you that it's NOT because they are publishing this book or because they've asked me to include these references. It's because the conference is that good! I would highly encourage you to consider attending.

[17] See endnote 1 again because I wasn't kidding.

[18] Ken Ham and Britt Beemer with Todd Hillard, *Already Gone: Why Your Kids Will Quit Church and What You Can Do to Stop It* (Green Forest, AR: Master Books, 2009).

[19] Granted, as you try new things with *your* teenagers, in *your* church, in *your* community, you're bound to swing and miss sometimes. Don't be discouraged if that happens! Instead, expect it and just be ready to try other ideas.

[20] As I write this, I haven't seen either movie. So this is not a statement about either movie specifically.

[21] This is another consequence of a post-Christian environment. In some parts of the country, going to a Christian movie may still have a cool factor to it. But there's a reason why you can count on two hands the number of theaters showing Christian movies in New England, for example.

[22] Case in point, literally a few days after writing that sentence, I had a 30-minute conversation about Noah, the Bible, and Jesus with two social workers I know who don't go to church much but are open to spiritual things. One of them *loved* the *Noah* movie, which led to the other one bringing up Rob Bell's recent appearance on "Super Soul Sunday" with Oprah. This led to a great conversation about the Bible, Jesus, and religion.

[23] Neil Fleming, *VARK: A Guide to Learning Styles*, 2001–2014, www.vark-learn.com/english/index.asp.

[24] Neil Fleming, "Table Five: Groups and the Percentages of V, A, R, and K Options Chosen," *VARK: A Guide to Learning Styles*, May 2013, www.vark-learn.com/english/page.asp?p=research.

[25] Neil Fleming, "Table Three: VARK Database: Distribution of Preferences," *VARK: A Guide to Learning Styles*, September 2012–December 2012, www.vark-learn.com/english/page.asp?p=research.

[26] Tim Stewart, *Dictionary of Christianese*, 2014, www.dictionaryofchristianese.com/list-of-words-by-alphabetical/.

[27] For a great resource, check out *How to Read the Bible for All It's Worth* by Gordon D. Fee and Doug Stuart (Zondervan, 2003).

[28] Rob Bell, *What We Talk About When We Talk About God* (New York: HarperOne/WORB Inc., 2013).

[29] Rob Bell, *Love Wins: A Book About Heaven, Hell, and the Fate of Every Person Who Ever Lived* (New York, NY: HarperCollins, 2011).

[30] This is exactly why when I quoted Rob Bell back in chapter 2, I gave him credit in the endnote, rather than naming him in the text. Note: I do find it extremely fun when people whom I know to be anti-Rob Bell comment on how fantastic a quote was, and then I get to watch the look on their faces when I reveal my source.

[31] Personally, I also loved Francis Chan and Preston Sprinkle's *Erasing Hell* (David C. Cook, 2011). *Erasing Hell* and *Love Wins* are fantastic to read side by side, as they will generate some amazing dialogue.

[32] Hemant Mehta, "An Atheist Walks into a Church…" *BeliefNet* (blog), August 2007, www.beliefnet.com/Faiths/2007/08/An-Atheist-Walks-Into-A-Church.aspx#2slhmalwjHHhkWuV.99.

[33] Hemant Mehta, *I Sold My Soul on eBay: Viewing Faith through an Atheist's Eyes* (Colorado Springs: WaterBrook Press, 2007), 110.

[34] Luke 14:25-33

[35] Dan Kimball, *They Like Jesus but Not the Church* (Grand Rapids, MI: Zondervan, 2007).

[36] John Ortberg, "The 'We' We Want to Be," *Leadership Journal*, Spring 2010, www.christianitytoday.com/le/2010/spring/wewanttobe.html.